D1636981

OPPORTUNITIES IN
BUSINESS
MANAGEMENT
CAREERS

Irene Place

Foreword by
Donald P. Jacobs
Dean
J.L. Kellogg Graduate School of Management

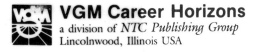 **VGM Career Horizons**
a division of *NTC Publishing Group*
Lincolnwood, Illinois USA

93 09318

Cover Photo Credits:

Front cover: upper left, U.S. Department of Health and Human Services photo; upper right, NTC photo; lower left, photo by Dennis Brack, Black Star, courtesy of Mead Corporation; lower right, the First National Bank of Chicago.

Back cover: upper left, Martha Johns photo; upper right, NTC photo; lower left and lower right, The First National Bank of Chicago.

Library of Congress Cataloging-in-Publication Data

Place, Irene Magdaline Glazik, 1912–
    Opportunities in business management careers / Irene Place.

        p.   cm. – (VGM opportunities series)
    ISBN 0-8442-8158-1 (hardbound) : $12.95. – ISBN 0-8442-8160-3
(softbound) : $9.95
    1. Business—Vocational guidance.   2. Management—Vocational
guidance.   I. Title.   II. Series.
HF5381.P585   1991
658'.0023'73–dc20   90-50738
                                                                          CIP

Published by VGM Career Horizons, a division of NTC Publishing Group.
©1991 by NTC Publishing Group, 4255 West Touhy Avenue,
Lincolnwood (Chicago), Illinois 60646-1975 U.S.A.
Manufactured in the United States of America.

1 2 3 4 5 6 7 8 9 VP 9 8 7 6 5 4 3 2 1

ABOUT THE AUTHOR

Irene Place is the coauthor of several business books: *Office Management, Management of the Electronic Office, Records Management: Controlling Business Information, Business Theory for Secretaries, The Road to Secretarial Success, Filing and Records Management,* and *College Secretarial Procedures.* She has written for professional journals and contributed chapters to nine business education yearbooks.

Irene Place is professor emeritus of business administration, School of Business at Portland State University. She previously taught on several university campuses including New York University (NYU) and the University of California (UCLA). She came to Portland State in 1966 from the Graduate School of Business Administration, the University of Michigan, where she was associate professor of office management. She received her B.A. from the University of Nebraska, her M.A. from Columbia Teachers College, and her Ed.D. from New York University.

Dr. Place was the first dean of the Institute for Certifying Secretaries (National Secretaries Association) 1950–52; na-

iii

tional chairman of the education committee, National Office Management Association (NOMA) from 1953–55, member of the board of the Detroit chapter of NOMA (1958–60), and chairman of its technical studies committee (1960–62). She has also been chairman of the education committee of the Detroit chapter of the Systems and Procedures Association (SPA) and editor of *Systems & Procedures,* the association's national magazine (1957–60). In 1968, she was the first woman to be awarded the Distinguished Service Award by the national association's International Awards Committee.

As president of the Portland chapter of Zonta International, she installed two chapters in Japan. She was president of the Portland metropolitan chapter of Pi Lambda Theta honorary education association. After being national vice-president (president-elect) of Delta Pi Epsilon honorary association in business education, she edited the association's research journal for $2^1/_2$ years. In 1983, she was chair of the residents' council of a 350-apartment retirement community and, in 1984–85, chaired the dedication program of a new 5^1/_2$ million, 92-apartment addition.

Dr. Place is an honorary member of Alpha Sigma Alpha, Phi Chi Theta, the National Secretaries Association, and the American Records Management Association. She has been the recipient of a Ford Foundation scholarship, a Rackham grant, an IBM internship, and an Oregon educational improvement grant.

ACKNOWLEDGMENT

The editors gratefully acknowledge Mariwyn Evans for her assistance in preparing this edition of the book.

FOREWORD

What is a manager?

All managers have a hand on the helm, regardless of where they practice their trade. The organization can be a business firm, a government agency, or a private, non-profite institution.

The goal can be profit or growth or both. It can be service, education, or promotion of health or the arts. It does not matter where, for whom, why—all managers are involved in the control, deployment, and use of resources—people, plants, materials, information, money.

All managers are decision makers. Managers are people who see to it that the work of the world gets done. Successful managers are those who, in preparation for their careers, have gained a working knowledge of the techniques and tools of management.

Good luck to you as you explore the many options offered by a career in business management.

> Donald P. Jacobs, Dean
> J. L. Kellogg Graduate School of Management

INTRODUCTION

It takes a special person to be a successful manager. Business managers must have the knowledge and self-confidence to formulate policy and direct the day-to-day operations of their companies. Good managers are able to motivate employees, organize a wide array of activities, and make informed decisions. The specific skills administrators need vary according to the industry, but basic business management techniques are common to all.

Education is key to the professional success of managers. Many pursue MBA degrees to develop the expertise required to do business in the increasingly complex, global marketplace. Business managers may find themselves analyzing budgets, preparing reports, or evaluating an employee's performance. Their varied duties require a balanced educational background.

Employment opportunities for managers vary by industry but should remain strong through the next decade. Some corporations have sought to cut costs by reducing managerial staff and increasing the responsibilities of individual managers. However, many industries, especially health care and the service sector, will have a growing need for new managers in the coming years.

Every business, from the corner restaurant to a large government agency, needs competent managers. Begin planning now for an exciting future in business management.

The Editors of VGM

CONTENTS

Management defined. Management hierarchy.
Opportunities. Management as a profession.
Management style.

Functional managers. The growth of the service
economy. Health services. Finance. Construction. Trade and retailing. Manufacturing. Transportation, public utilities, and communication.
Education. Self-employment. Multinational opportunities. Preparation.

Earnings of managers. Fringe benefits. Employment security. How far is up?

CHAPTER 1

WHAT IS MANAGEMENT?

The United States is an industrially developed country with sophisticated government, business, social, educational, and service organizations. The leaders of these organizations are managers and are called by various names such as boss, director, department head, principal, chief executive officer (CEO), president, branch manager, executive, and administrator.

If becoming a business manager interests you, this book is for you. It describes the wide variety of managerial opportunities, from top-level management positions to middle and beginning management jobs. The focus of the book is entry- and middle-level jobs where most young people find the greatest opportunity.

MANAGEMENT DEFINED

Management activities are generally similar from company to company. However, privileges, salaries, and opportunities differ, as do individual managers' abilities and levels of responsibility. Managers plan and control major functions of an organization. They try to anticipate opportunities and changes, and then lead the way. Their resources are traditionally described as the five M's of management: men (and women!), money, materials, methods, and machines.

To make their resources productive, managers organize, coordinate, direct, and develop them. For example, they organize groups of employees and assign duties to them. This creates communication (information) systems, production systems, and distribution systems. A good manager is able to turn a department or task force into a highly productive team that strives as a unit to reach company goals.

All management jobs include planning, organizing, directing, and controlling. The degree to which each of these functions becomes part of a manager's responsibility depends on two things: (1) the level and extent of the manager's authority as a decision-maker, and (2) the nature and size of the organization. In large organizations, managers specialize in different tasks such as keeping track of the company's finances or creating products or services that the company can market. In a small owner-operated company with only a few employees, the owner will probably manage many or all of these functions.

Regardless of the size of an organization or the level of management responsibility, one basic task is human resource development. Managers who understand and respect the importance of the human element in management get the best results, although the degree to which they work directly with employees and the public will depend on their particular jobs. Some managers, like those in schools, restaurants, and social service agencies, are in constant touch with the public, while those working with research or publications may deal with only a few in-house associates.

MANAGEMENT HIERARCHY

As the size and complexity of a company's operations increase, so do its layers of management. Giant corporations may have ten or more layers—generally classified as top managers, middle managers, and supervisors.

Careless use of such words as supervisor, manager, executive, and administrator has caused some confusion in understanding each manager's level. Supervisors, or junior managers, plan and schedule day-to-day employee operations. They direct every type of production and service activity in an organization—including data processing, records management, security, and shipping. For example, in a department store, a supervisor might oversee several sales clerks, keep inventory records, and see that merchandise is replaced as needed.

Middle Managers

Middle managers function between top management and supervisors. In other words, they report to top managers, and supervisors report to them. In large organizations, middle managers might be responsible for branch plants or regional developments. A middle manager of chain stores, for example, might be responsible for all the stores in a region, such as the Midwest.

Doctors, lawyers, engineers, accountants, and other professional or technical people are not usually considered managers because they do not spend much time on management activities. When employed by companies, they are usually classified as staff members and work in advisory capacities where they use their specialized knowledge and skills.

In some companies, one outcome of recent efforts to increase productivity and lower operating costs has been a reduction in the number of middle managers. The increased emphasis on a team approach to projects has also lessened the need for mid-level managers.

A Management Hierarchy

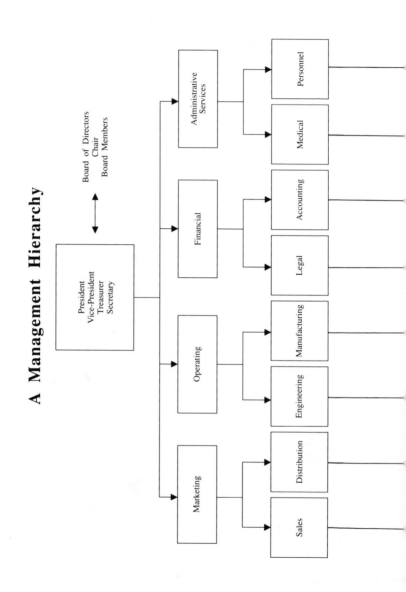

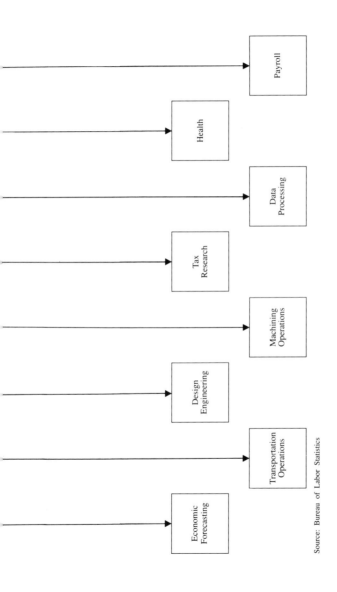

Source: Bureau of Labor Statistics

Top Managers

Supervisors and middle managers are production oriented. They make decisions relating to personnel, materials, and procedures. Top managers are policy oriented. They chart an organization's course and set overall goals. Their ranks include the board of directors, the CEO, and the vice-presidents of major departments such as production, finance, and sales. Top managers analyze large amounts of information that come from within the company and from the world outside. They must decide what impact political, technological, and social trends will have on their organizations.

OPPORTUNITIES

There was a time when a young person had to own a business in order to be a manager, but that time is long past. Now, the majority of management opportunities open to young people looking for leadership roles are in corporations. Some people prefer less competitive and more structured situations in government or in family-owned businesses, but the trend is to work in a large corporation, although management is not usually an entry-level position. How, then, do you get started?

Some people find entry-level jobs with good companies and move upward on a career path from general employee to unit supervisor to department manager, and so on. Some look for companies with active management training programs and enroll in them. Others major in business administration or political science and, after graduation, start as management trainees. Many begin in other occupations. Many school administrators, for example, began as teachers; store managers, as sales people; and marketing executives, as field representatives.

To be considered for management positions, employees must prove that they can do their assigned work, maintain good relations with others, and take on more responsibility. This may mean putting in overtime voluntarily, participating in meetings constructively, and taking training courses willingly. Training opportunities may also include accepting temporary assignments in other company units or serving as an assistant to another manager.

Most people make their own job opportunities by watching and preparing for new responsibilities. Being knowledgeable enough to seize an opportunity is as essential as getting the chance.

MANAGEMENT AS A PROFESSION

The expansion of business operations in this country and throughout the world has complicated the role of the modern manager. Government regulations, Senate hearings, new technology, and the development of diversified and multinational corporations make professional preparation for careers in management highly desirable. Management has become an area of specialization.

A professional manager is a salaried expert, trained by education and experience to manage any type of organization—be it a government agency, a computer company, a restaurant, a hospital, or a motel. Although they are only salaried employees, professionals make decisions that affect the total organization—the prices consumers pay and the dividends stockholders receive.

Management is now recognized as a profession with standard practices and a code of ethics. Some think of it as a science consisting of definite subjects that managers can learn, such as accounting, computer technology, group dynamics, analytical problem solving, and risk taking. Others regard it as an applied art because it takes skill to develop and motivate the human resources involved.

Shareholders or business owners hire professional managers to run an enterprise on their behalf. To survive, a company must market saleable goods and services at the right price and quality. Management can achieve this goal only if it employs productive people who are satisfied with the company's working conditions. When a company's management fails, the market value of the company's stock falls. The enterprise then becomes prey for corporate "raiders" who buy poorly managed organizations that have good potential. When that happens, top managers of the raided company are usually replaced.

Effective leaders are dynamic people. They create an atmosphere of change with such enthusiasm and conviction that they excite others and stimulate them to work harder. Consequently, they often achieve objectives that originally seemed out of reach.

Sam Walton, founder and chair of Wal-Mart, Inc., exemplifies the management style of the 1990s. Starting with one small store in rural Arkansas, he has built a retail empire based on quality products and good service at low prices.

Walton maintains that most of his ideas are not original, claiming that he has borrowed a little from everyone. The key to his success seems to rest in his recognition of the value of service and his ability to motivate employees to provide that service on an ongoing basis. Walton often drops in unannounced at his retail outlets to ensure that high-quality service remains.

Mr. Walton is an outstanding manager. But he and all the other managers across the country have one thing in common. They all have businesses to run. When they are effective, their companies survive, provide jobs, and retain their share of the market.

The person who has the natural ability to manage an organization effectively under varying conditions is unusual. Some people have better aptitude for managing than others—just as some lawyers, doctors, ministers, and professors have more talent than their colleagues. This does not mean, however, that natural, charismatic leaders can disregard the theory and fundamentals of management education. Even born leaders need to learn how to use their resources effectively. Professional managers need to know management theory, if for no other reason than to appreciate the problems, philosophies, and principles of earlier managers. Even talented leaders are likely to encounter some difficulty in moving from one managerial level to another. In this situation, acquired skills, increased knowledge, and an understanding of behavioral psychology are valuable assets.

Management Scope

You may have noticed that nearly everyone takes care of (manages) something: children, pets, money, property. Of course, professional management goes beyond just taking care of people or things. Through special knowledge and administrative skills, managers try to maximize results, to get the most out of both material and human resources.

MAXIMIZING RESULTS

Another word for maximizing results is *synergism*—achieving a total result that is greater than the sum of the parts. Stated differently, resources are more valuable when they interact than when they remain separate. Synergism, therefore, is a desirable goal for all types of managers.

As an example of maximizing results through effective management, consider how two people manage their savings. One person stores the money in a box and buries it for safekeeping. The other invests it and increases its value. This simple illustration shows how one manager may conserve resources even though they may depreciate in value over time. The effective manager does something to improve the value of resources.

SOCIOECONOMIC IMPACT

Since management is a means of making progress and of producing results through others, it provides jobs, goods, and services that affect us all. As managers become involved in social and economic problems such as inflation, minority rights, and public accountability, they affect employment and life-styles. As business and government managers become involved in international relations, they affect world commerce, natural resources, and the total health of our society.

A WORLD ECONOMY

The trend is toward a global economy. Firms from Italy and Japan have branches in the United States, and American firms have branches in countries all over the world. This trend, facilitated by airplanes and communication satellites, gives managers a new role—leaders in world problems and human rights.

Some of the problems that the world faces can be alleviated or even solved by the experienced leadership and judgment found in upper management levels. Even though profit making and competition remain at the heart of business management, responsible leaders recognize the dignity of labor and the importance of human rights everywhere. Business leaders today must examine their value systems in the larger context of world problems. They are becoming more aware of the need to preserve resources and to develop a better world for everyone. Today's managers have a unique opportunity. They can work to maximize results and to help solve some of the world's urgent problems.

What's in it for you? You will find a whole lifetime of exciting challenges to leave the world just a little better than you found it. But you must get the right education, acquire meaningful management experiences, and be willing to work and to assume responsibility.

MANAGEMENT STYLE

What is the best way to manage: authoritarian, permissive, consultative? Should one tell employees what to do and how to do it? Or should one take time to confer with them? There are zealots, pragmatists, and by-the-book managers. The issue of management style is a lively one because a manager's style does make a difference in how people react and work together. The current trend is toward a participative approach and a group-think style.

Which style gets the best results?

Most experts believe that, to some degree, a person's management style is dictated by his or her personality. At the same time, a good manager must adapt his or her natural style to fit the personalities of employees and the demands of the work being supervised. For example, accounting work is very detailed and must be performed in prescribed ways. Likewise, those in the accounting field are generally attracted to it because of its order and predictability. Therefore, a manager might tend to use a more autocratic style to ensure that all work is done according to the required rules. On the other hand, a manager of a group of architects might find a participatory style more suitable because architects must be creative in order to achieve their design goals. This manager would need to give employees freedom to try new ideas and find the best solutions.

The Team Approach

In the United States, managers pay special attention to creating environments where employees can grow and participate. The modern trend is to involve workers in planning goals and procedures that affect the company's progress. To help employees gain skill and confidence in group participation, managers experiment with team approaches—weekly meetings, ad hoc committees, and performance evaluation conferences.

Some managers have learned that a good way to get employee cooperation is by using the team approach. Employees learn to share ideas, overcome negative attitudes, and improve interpersonal communication skills. However, many managers still have to learn how to use the team approach effectively.

CHAPTER 2

EMPLOYMENT OUTLOOK

It is hard to describe a manager's opportunities because they are so diverse. In 1988 there were about 12.2 million management jobs. The Bureau of Labor Statistics predicts that by the year 2000 there will be 14.8 million management jobs, although some companies may cut costs by reducing the number of managers.

FUNCTIONAL MANAGERS

Large organizations are usually divided into major functions such as production, personnel, finance, sales and marketing, and research and development.

Production managers see that the company's products are turned out efficiently. They establish production standards, design workstations, select and maintain equipment, and coordinate all the resources involved. They often have engineering backgrounds.

Table 2.1
Increase in Management Jobs

Occupation	Employment— 1988	Employment— 2000	Percent Increase
All managers	12,104	14,762	22
Administrative services	217	274	26
Communications, Transportation, Utilities	167	194	16
Construction	187	236	26
Education	320	400	19
Engineering	258	341	32
Financial	673	802	19
Food service	560	721	29
General	3,030	3,509	16
Government	69	71	3
Industrial	215	254	18
Marketing	406	511	26
Personnel	171	208	22
Property	225	267	19
Purchasing	252	289	14
All other	1,925	2,515	30
Management support	3,428	4,187	22

Personnel, or human resource, managers help to hire, train, and motivate employees for all departments of a company. (Some companies call this function "industrial relations.") This position involves maintaining personnel records, interviewing, testing, orienting, counseling, and evaluating employees. If unions are involved, it may also include labor negotiations.

Finance managers plan and coordinate the receiving, safeguarding, spending, investing, and allocating of funds. They also create records to account for the use of those funds.

Sales managers are concerned with plans, campaigns, and programs for selling the company's products. Persons without much formal education are likely to find better initial opportunities in sales than in other areas of management, especially if they get along well with people. Some companies rotate salespeople into different jobs to learn various developmental phases of their products. For those with managerial potential, job rotation provides an opportunity to understand the company as a whole and to learn through hands-on experience.

Research and development managers need to have a technical grasp of a company's product development as well as administrative ability. Management positions in this area are usually filled by scientific personnel. Often those who progress in research departments have doctoral degrees in science or engineering. Top jobs include director of research, director of new product development, and chief engineer.

Variety of Environments

American business is classified in U.S. Department of Labor publications by the type of industry. Due to limited space, this chapter covers only those classifications with good growth potential. Management opportunities in farming, forestry, mining, and fishing, are, therefore, not discussed. Areas with high potential at this writing include services such as finance, law, health services, insurance, retail, and self-employment.

THE GROWTH OF THE SERVICE ECONOMY

The U.S. Department of Labor predicts that much of the country's economic growth during the 1990s will be in the service sector. The service sector encompasses many levels of jobs, from accountant and lawyer to hospital worker and waitress. Any job that produces a service instead of a concrete product falls under this heading.

In 1988, the number of jobs in the service sector (16 million) was already higher than the number in manufacturing (9 million). By the year 2000, four out of every five jobs is expected to be in the service sector.

Because many service-sector businesses require a large number of employees, the growth of the service sector should offer increased opportunities for management. Some of this growth may be offset by better productivity made possible by computers.

As these changes take place, the traditional managerial hierarchy will flatten out because businesses will need fewer line supervisors and middle managers. This consolidation, along with new management techniques such as team approaches, will turn managers into mentors and coaches rather than production "taskmasters."

HEALTH SERVICES

Management opportunities in health services are projected to grow as the number of senior citizens increases. Health services include hospitals, nursing homes, and personal care centers. Some of these institutions are multimillion dollar organizations with hundreds of staff members and residents. Attempts to control spiraling health-care costs have lead to a slightly lower growth rate in top-level health-care jobs. However, the four fastest growing

Table 2.2
Growth in Service Industries

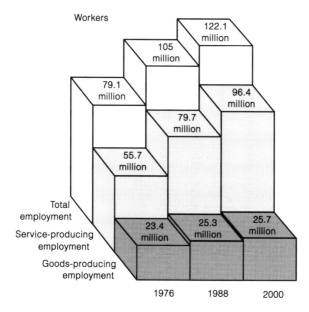

Source: Bureau of Labor Statistics

jobs listed by the Bureau of the Census are all in the health-care area.

Universities have introduced master's degree programs for hospital administrators. Administrators for other types of health-service units come from nursing, the ministry, special public health programs, sociology departments, gerontology courses, and special community college programs.

Health care is becoming big business, and many new management opportunities are emerging. These include positions in state health maintenance agencies such as the American Association of Homes for the Aging (AAHA) and group medical centers. These centers may include psychiatric, emergency, outpatient, and rehabilitation care for people who do not require constant attention.

Current occupational statistics compiled by the U.S. Department of Labor report 177,000 health service administrators in 1988. Through the year 2000, opportunities for health-care managers are expected to increase much faster than the average for all occupations. There are also growing management opportunities in related industries such as drug manufacturing and health-care products.

FINANCE

Companies in the finance industry include the savings and loan associations, brokerage firms, commercial and savings banks, and investment houses. Large corporations have major financial departments. Some of them are responsible for maintaining retirement plans and investing millions of dollars of employee retirement funds. Real estate and insurance employment ranges from large corporations to small, independent companies which offer management opportunities for those interested in working for smaller organizations.

The Bureau of Labor Statistics reports that there were 673,000 financial managers and 225,000 real estate managers in 1988. It estimates that employment in the financial, real estate, and insurance area should increase by 1.3 percent every year during the 1990s.

CONSTRUCTION

The construction industry includes many small companies which subcontract to large ones. About 4.9 million of the gainfully employed workers in this country are in the construction business. Of these, 187,000 were managers in 1988. Specializations in the construction industry include commercial, residential, hospital, educational, public utility, chemical, industrial, public highway, and miscellaneous public service companies. Construction jobs are expected to rise 18 percent in the 1990s. Slower residential construction in the second half of the decade will be offset by more commercial building.

TRADE AND RETAILING

General merchandise stores employ thousands of buyers and department heads as well as home-office and branch managers. Chain restaurants, cafés, bars, and nightclubs also account for a good many management opportunities. These opportunities will continue to grow as long as incomes remain stable because working women are adding to the number of people dining out and vacationing. The number of retail store managers is also expected to increase because of the growth in chain operations.

Overall employment in retail and wholesale trade is expected to increase by 27 percent during the 1990s, according to the U.S. Department of Labor, Bureau of Labor Statistics. Over half of new retail jobs (approximately 12 million) will be in eating and drinking places. Employment opportunities for marketing, advertising, and public relations managers are also expected to grow much faster than average in the next decade.

Because Americans love to shop, the retail and wholesale industries provide many management positions. These industries are excellent training grounds for prospective managers because running a store is like running a total business system. Higher level opportunities, however, are usually strongest in the company's home office. Merchandising continues to be a growth industry, although at an average rate.

MANUFACTURING

Approximately 6 percent of all American workers are employed in manufacturing durable and nondurable goods. Examples of durable goods include furniture and fixtures (lumber, wood, stone, clay, and glass products); metal goods (smelting and refining products); machinery and transportation equipment (automobiles, aircraft, railroad cars, and boats); and military equipment. Examples of nondurable goods include food, soaps and cosmetics, textiles and apparel, printing and publishing products, chemicals, rubber, leather, and petroleum products.

Manufacturing companies range from small individual proprietorships to huge corporations such as General Motors, Ford Motor Company, and International Business Machines (IBM). The U.S. Department of Labor expects manufacturing employment to decline by about 4 percent during the 1990s because of gains in productivity. Not all manufacturing industries will decline, however. Commercial printing, computer equipment, and medical instruments are three areas that are expected to prosper in the next ten years.

TRANSPORTATION, PUBLIC UTILITIES, AND COMMUNICATION

Transportation and public utilities employ about 4.4 percent of the country's work force and are projected to experience average growth through the year 2000. Transportation firms, including airlines; bus, taxi, and rent-a-car companies; railroads; and shipping and trucking companies are expected to grow nearly twice as fast as the division as a whole. Public utilities, such as gas, electric, and water providers, will have slow, but steady, growth. Only communication, including telephone and telegraph companies and radio and television stations, will decline.

Because the services these companies provide are vitally important to the public, their operations are subject to government regulation. The Interstate Commerce Commission, the Federal Power Commission, and the Civil Aeronautics Administration review their rates and issue various permits and licenses. As a result, companies in this classification have special management problems. But their overall management activities are basically the same as in other industries.

EDUCATION

There are about 1,300 four-year colleges and universities and nearly 1,000 two-year colleges in the country. There are thousands of public grade and high schools, as well as private schools. All these institutions need administrators. Education is big business.

School administrative positions include principal, department head, dean, president, and provost. The many types of vice-presidents include finance, student affairs, and administration. Also, every state has a board of education, and local communities have school superintendents. In 1988, 320,000 people were employed as educational administrators. In 1988, 17 percent of those working as managers had only a high school education, while 61 percent had completed at least four years of college.

Growth in educational management positions depends somewhat on population shifts. The employment of elementary and secondary-school administrators is projected to increase at the

Table 2.3
Comparative Growth in Businesses

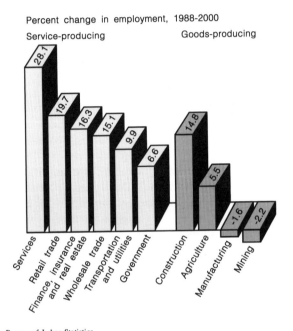

Percent change in employment, 1988-2000

Service-producing   Goods-producing

Services — 28.1
Retail trade — 19.7
Finance, insurance and real estate — 16.3
Wholesale trade — 15.1
Transportation and utilities — 9.9
Government — 6.6
Construction — 14.8
Agriculture — 5.5
Manufacturing — -1.6
Mining — -2.2

Source: Bureau of Labor Statistics

average rate of all occupations through the year 2000, although the present decline in the school age population is reversing.

SELF-EMPLOYMENT

Self-employment offers another opportunity for those interested in moving into management. While larger enterprises offer more opportunities for management advancement, self-employment may be the best answer for those with strong entrepreneurial skills or those without the conventional educational requirements for management.

The growth of the service sector has prompted an increase in the number of small businesses. As a result, self-employment is growing. In 1988, 15.3 percent of managers were self-employed; by the year 2000 that number is expected to reach 17.8 percent.

As business operations become more complex, the need for salaried managers is expected to continue because of the growing dependency of business organizations and government agencies on professional managers. Management jobs are projected to increase about as fast as average for all jobs through the year 2000.

However, according to the U.S. Department of Labor the speed of growth in management jobs may vary significantly with the health of the particular industry. At the same time, unemployment among managers is expected to reach only 1.9 percent, compared with an overall rate of 5.5 percent.

MULTINATIONAL OPPORTUNITIES

The economic trend is away from national self-sufficiency toward global interdependency. U.S. corporations invest in foreign countries, and foreign companies invest in the United States.

In 1987, U.S. companies had invested $926,042 million in affiliations with foreign companies. Companies with overseas operations represent the entire range of manufacturing and service business. Car manufacturers, textile companies, and banking and investment firms are just a few examples of companies that offer management opportunities in foreign countries.

In many cases, a foreign branch of a U.S. firm will be headed by a national of the country in which the branch is located, someone who knows the language and the customs of the area.

This is particularly true in joint venture efforts. However, a portion of every foreign office staff is usually composed of U.S. managers. In addition, there are often management-level opportunities for those who coordinate communications between foreign subsidiaries and the main office.

At the same time, foreign investment in the United States is at an all-time high, increasing 25 times in the last two decades. According to the Department of Commerce, foreign companies invested $58 billion in the United States, in 1988 alone. While a portion of this money is invested in the stock and money markets, foreign companies also are opening manufacturing plants and buying real estate throughout the United States.

Just as U.S. firms often employ foreign managers abroad, non-U.S. firms hire American managers for their operations. Working for a foreign firm may offer exciting opportunities to travel. At the same time, it requires special sensitivity to adapt to the management and business styles of those from different cultures.

International commerce generates many exciting management opportunities. As an inducement for managers to work in foreign countries, most companies offer a variety of incentives. Some provide housing plus utilities, travel opportunities, and "hardship" bonuses.

PREPARATION

Managers working in foreign countries should possess a few special qualifications because they represent American culture wherever they work. Some of these qualifications are:

1. A tolerance for different customs and a willingness to learn about them
2. Fluency in several languages

3. Knowledge about different political systems, national groups, and international law
4. Knowledge about world geography and demographic movements
5. Knowledge of the metric system and currency exchange
6. A proven ability to adapt to new situations
7. Independence and self-reliance
8. Physical and emotional health
9. Lack of prejudice with regard to race, religion, culture, or business practices
10. A good basic education

Those who participate in world commerce must continue their educations for a lifetime.

CHAPTER 3

MANAGEMENT EARNINGS

As you can see, management is a challenging and often rewarding experience. It offers opportunities to use your knowledge in
shaping the direction of a company, a product, and the careers of
other workers.

Management is also a rewarding profession on the financial
side. One often reads about six- and seven-figure salaries earned
by superstar athletes, newscasters, and television personalities.
Overlooked is the fact that an athlete's career is short-lived, often
ending by the time the player is 35 or 40 years old.

Professional managers, on the other hand, have a sustained
earning power that often lasts for several decades, and they are
usually assured of substantial retirement incomes for the rest of
their lives. Some executives even stay on as consultants and
members of the board of directors.

EARNINGS OF MANAGERS

Managers generally earn more than nonmanagers. In fact, top-
level executives are among the highest paid workers in the country.
They are highly paid because their leadership skills directly affect
company growth, economic survival, and internal vitality. Man-

Table 3.1
Weekly Managerial Earnings

Occupation	Median	Median/men	Median/women
Executive	$547	$682	$265
Public administration	550	617	476
Protective service	584	N/A	N/A
Financial	630	788	487
Personnel	666	785	563
Purchasing	644	709	N/A
Marketing	702	814	503
Education	617	757	499
Health	587	743	535
Property	424	516	355
Management-related	501	610	426

Source: Bureau of Labor Statistics

agers make decisions, develop resources, set policies, take risks, and motivate their associates who may include financial backers.

Management earnings vary with company size. In fact, company size is the single largest factor affecting compensation, with an executive in a large company earning as much as ten times the salary of an executive in a small firm.

Salaries also vary from industry to industry. For example, restaurant, cafeteria, and bar managers average $26,000 per year; financial managers, $32,800; and hotel managers, $30,000. A recent *Salary Survey Report* published by the College Placement Council indicated that the average annual starting salary offered to college seniors ranged from $20,942 in business administration to $21,732 in marketing, $24,342 in accounting, and $26,003 in management information. High salaries are generally offered in finance and manufacturing.

Salary levels vary substantially based on length of service, level of responsibility, and location of the firm. The estimated median salary of general managers and executives was $38,700 in 1988. Many earned well over $52,000. A recent survey of top corporations revealed that over 150 chief executive officers received base salaries of over one million dollars. With additional compensation, such as pension, stock options, and so forth, total earnings could be much higher.

FRINGE BENEFITS

Success in management may be measured by title or status and by material rewards such as salary, bonuses, and stock options. It may include special privileges such as vacations, or use of company vehicles or other facilities. Such fringe benefits are sometimes called "perks."

Differences in fringe benefits among companies depend on size of company, location, type of business, whether the business is unionized, and the philosophy of its management. Programs may include the following:

bonuses	professional association dues
coffee breaks	profit-sharing
disability payments	sabbatical leaves
group insurance	savings plans
maternity leave	sick leave
military leave	stock options
paid holidays	tuition-assisted education
pensions	union service leave
	vacations

A few companies are innovative about their benefit programs and try new approaches. For example, one company promotes the "cultural environment" of its employees and discusses employee self-renewal opportunities that will improve minds and attitudes. Although its benefits plan includes most of the items listed above, focus is on the following provisions:

1. A promotion system that gives full-time employees first chance before outside recruitments are considered
2. An extensive educational program with over 400 courses held in the company educational center
3. A profit-sharing plan for full-time employees
4. Three health plans from which to choose
5. Psychological and family counseling
6. Educational leaves
7. Graduated retirement plans

According to the Bureau of Labor Statistics, 65 percent of managerial personnel employed in medium and large firms during 1988 received pension benefits, 20 percent received profit sharing, and 18 percent received cash bonuses. However, only 3 percent of managerial employees received stock options.

In *The American Almanac of Jobs and Salaries,* author John W. Wright cites a 1985 survey by the executive placement firm Korn/Ferry. The study demonstrates the value of benefits.

Employee Investment Plans

The board of directors and stockholders of a company may authorize that shares of a company's common stock be made available to salaried employees as part of a company-sponsored employee savings plan. Employees may invest deductions directly from their pay, and the company may match up to 50 percent of the investments. This matching is usually restricted to 2 to 4 percent of an employee's total pay, and company contributions are

Table 3.2
Benefits for Executives, by Level

Benefit	*Top Executive*	*Midlevel Manager*	*Lower-level Manager*
Base Salary	$300,000	$100,000	$40,000
Annual Bonus	50% to 100% of salary	40% to 80% of salary	25% to 50% of salary
Insurance	3 times base salary	$1^1/_2$ times base salary	$1^1/_2$ times base salary
Retirement Salary	65% of average salary for past 5 years	40% to 50% of average salary for past 5 years	40% to 50% of average salary for past 5 years

invested only in company shares. Employees usually pay less than the market price for the stock.

Financial Award Plans

Another benefit plan is a special long-term incentive program for officers and key executives only. This program reflects a growing practice in many industries to recognize and reward key executives who have major responsibilities for determining future performance and growth of the organization, often in a highly competitive international setting. These plans try to reward executives commensurate with their achievements in meeting major financial and service objectives. Awards may be in cash or stocks. Cash awards are payable in a lump sum or annual installments over a period not exceeding five years. Executives may defer payments to later years, to be paid with interest.

One year, one of the country's large corporations aggregated nearly $3 million for distribution to its key executives. Usually each executive is eligible for an award only periodically—perhaps once in five years. A committee composed of outside directors in cooperation with outside consultants selects award recipients.

It is maintained that such plans motivate executive performance and help a company retain a high-quality management team capable of leading the firm in a growing, complex, and volatile economic environment. The following sampling shows the possible size of executive cash awards in large corporations and how such awards affect salaries of highly paid officials.

Basic Salary	+	Cash Award	=	Total
$375,000		$325,000		$700,000
240,000		260,000		500,000

In addition to cash awards, key executives may receive hundreds of shares of company stock for outstanding performance. Annual reports show that top executives often own, personally or in family trusts, from 100 to 50,000 shares. A not-to-be-overlooked benefit for them is that they may also consult company tax lawyers and specialists when preparing federal and state income tax reports, and planning financial matters.

One factor that has recently influenced management benefit packages was a proposed law that would have penalized companies that offered dramatically different levels of benefits to their management and regular employees. While the proposed law was defeated, it did prompt many corporations to equalize benefits offered to managers and other employees. Managers are still much more likely to receive certain special benefits—such as stock options and bonuses—than are regular employees. But in the areas of vacation, health programs, and other, more common benefits, the differences in benefit packages are seldom significant today.

Retirement Plan

In most American corporations, an employee who retires at 65 or older with one or more years of service (or at 60 with 15 or more years of service) will receive a monthly income for life in addition to Social Security. Examples of how these incomes are computed follow:

1. $18 times the number of years of service: $18 × 10years = $180 monthly
2. $1\frac{1}{2}$ percent of compensation for every year of service: 1.5 (.015) × $800 (average wage) × 12 years (years of service) = $144.00
3. A pension benefit calculated by subtracting one-twelfth of 50 percent of the estimated Social Security Benefit.

There are many such formulas, some determined by the executive committee or negotiated with a union. Early retirement at a reduced retirement income is becoming popular because of fast technological changes and job obsolescence; employee burnout from stressful jobs, complex decision making, psychological fatigue; and the need to trim "fat" from organizations. Many firms are encouraging employees to retire after age 55 with 15 years of service or at any age with 30 years of service.

EMPLOYMENT SECURITY

Managers not only earn more on average than most workers, they are also less likely to be unemployed than the average U.S. worker. The Bureau of Labor Statistics projects that unemployment among all categories of managers—except construction managers—will be low or very low throughout the next decade. While current trends toward reducing management overhead may affect these figures slightly, a manager is more likely to have a secure job than the average employee.

Of course, managers are sometimes fired or laid off in corporate restructurings. However, a manager is more likely to receive another job offer or assistance in finding new employment than is the average worker. Likewise, executives nearing age sixty or older are often offered early retirement packages with incentives as a way to reduce management ranks. Thus, executives are less likely than the average worker to be left in financial straits by a layoff.

HOW FAR IS UP?

After reading this information about fringe benefits, the young reader may feel like a mountain climber standing at the base of a pinnacle yet to be scaled. How far up can he or she get?

Obviously the top benefits described in this chapter are achieved by only a few who carry the burden of keeping the organization profitable and competitive. They are the captains of the ships of industry, and their decision-making responsibilities in the world's complex economy are terrific. Only a few have the ability to function at the top tiers of leadership.

Be reminded, if you are not so inclined or qualified, that there are thousands of leadership roles between line supervision and top management where you can make satisfying contributions. There are plenty of management opportunities for everyone because wherever people work together, leaders are needed. If you enjoy leading, prepare for the role. If you prepare conscientiously, you will surely achieve some measure of success in a field that pleases you. A 79-year-old former executive officer of a large oil company was asked, "As a man acutely aware of what it takes to be successful, what advice would you offer?" He answered:

Well, I'd say the most important point is to never, never lose your enthusiasm. No matter what you do, do it with enthusiasm. I enjoy my work. It's exhilarating. I also think I have a receptive mind and a good memory. I listen to people, and from listening I get a lot of ideas. I learn of opportunities that perhaps other people would miss. . . . it's a combination of many things. I've always been a great optimist, although I try to temper it with a certain amount of conservatism and realism. But if you approach everything in a negative fashion, you'll never get anywhere.

All in all, I would say that people should try to do a better job than anyone else has done before and to do it with zest. I suppose my ambition in life is to leave the world a little better than when I found it.

CHAPTER 4

EDUCATION

Although most managers have studied at colleges and universities, many of those who work in small stores or are self-employed have relatively little formal education. On the other hand, many managers working in high-tech industries and as senior executives in large firms have degrees in engineering, law, and graduate business administration. An education, if well assimilated, opens doors in a wide range of organizations, although much can be learned about human behavior and group dynamics from the "school of experience."

There is a trend to employ graduates of liberal arts programs because managers recognize the need for generalists as well as specialists. Another source for management recruits is the army. Some claim to prefer young ex-army officers to MBAs, especially if the officers are West Point graduates. The military gives personnel responsibility faster than many civilian organizations, and military officers learn to work with and depend on people around them.

The West Point of American management schools is the Graduate School of Business Administration at Harvard University. At Harvard, students may earn an M.B.A. in two years. Those who acquire the degree often have an undergraduate degree in engineering, science, economics, or liberal arts. Which combination

Increasing Number of Workers with College Background

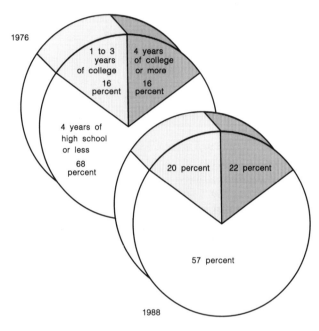

1976

1 to 3
years
of college
16
percent

4 years
of college
or more
16
percent

4 years of
high school
or less
68
percent

20 percent

22 percent

57 percent

1988

Source: Bureau of Labor Statistics

is the most desirable depends upon individual goals. Many other universities and colleges throughout the country use the Harvard program as a model.

Business education at the collegiate level began in the latter part of the nineteenth century. The first collegiate program, called the Wharton School of Finance and Economy, was started in 1881 at the University of Pennsylvania. Today, America has more than

2,700 colleges and 700 collegiate business schools and departments of business administration.

Speaking at the 1989 American Assembly of Collegiate Schools of Business (AACSB), Bob Jaedicke, dean of Stanford's business school, suggested that management educators must look outward to the marketplace to find better ways to prepare managers for leadership. Jaedicke noted that new work markets move faster and with more flexibility than current academic models and that students and midcareer managers must prepare for an era of global business. Jaedicke suggested that students become less specialized and concentrate more on major business themes, such as global markets, nonmarket forces, the management of technology, and management ethics.

Annual salaries for MBA graduates may go as high as $100,000. However, a recent article in *U.S. News and World Report* stated that the average annual starting salary for a graduate of one of the top 25 MBA programs was approximately $49,000.

MIDMANAGEMENT PROGRAMS

Those who cannot afford to spend four to six years in college to prepare for leadership roles in business and government may choose associate degree programs in community colleges. Such programs are designed to prepare people for first-line management (supervisory) jobs and are an effective way to begin a management career. Two appealing characteristics of this approach are:

1. *A shorter preparation period.* This enables you to start to work with a good company sooner, even though not at a high level. Nevertheless, you get experience sooner, and your company may help finance your education.
2. *Lower cost.* Fees are generally lower at a two-year school than at a four-year one.

As many companies help employees earn a degree after they are employed, community college midmanagement students should be careful to select courses that will transfer to four-year schools. Two-year schools offer many nontransfer courses that are sometimes designated as vocational or technical courses. Typical business transfer courses are accounting, computer programming, communications, principles of management, mathematics of business, statistics, data processing, marketing, and finance.

According to *Multinational Business* (Winter 1989), a number of U.S. institutions are finding a growing niche in serving the needs of executives returning to school. These programs, which are often taught on evenings and weekends, include both B.A., MBA, and other related degrees. These programs, according to *Multinational Business,* are much more likely than traditional programs to have curriculum driven by market demand.

BEGINNING MANAGERS

Inexperienced young people rarely enter management positions directly from college unless they go into family-owned firms or start their own businesses. However, most large companies do recruit management trainees from college campuses. Interviewers check a student's interests, extracurricular activities, judgment, ambitions, maturity, and management potential. A few companies give tests. Some look for special skills in engineering, accounting, finance, or the law. Trainee positions become stepping stones to management positions.

Here are some helpful hints for those entering training programs:

1. Get a general education, preferably a college degree, before specializing. The MBA is considered the specialized degree for managers.

2. Acquire specific knowledge in accounting, finance, economics, world markets, organization, production, group dynamics, and computer technology.
3. Be willing to work and study hard.
4. Improve your decision-making techniques, and keep track of lessons learned from experience.
5. Don't be afraid of new ideas; try new approaches; think up alternate solutions to problems.
6. Learn to get along with all types of people; learn how to help them change.
7. Keep your career on track; periodically reexamine your goals and ways to reach them.
8. Assume responsibility willingly but thoughtfully.
9. Don't kid yourself; face your shortcomings, and decide what to do about them.

There are all kinds of good management opportunities out there. Every organization is looking for competent, level-headed leaders. Your first step is to find opportunities that match your interests and capabilities. Then study, learn from experience as well as theory, and make your knowledge work for you.

THE MBA

Increasingly, those who hope to climb executive ladders are choosing to acquire MBA (master, business administration) or similar advanced management degrees. If a college degree was once the mark of a person on the fast track, the MBA has replaced it as the indicator of great things to come. The number of MBAs rose from 21,400 in 1970 to 70,000 in 1987 and is expected to increase just as rapidly in the decade ahead. One-third of the MBAs in 1987 were women. At the same time, a recent study of

500 corporations, done by the University of Michigan, found that demand for MBA graduates has slackened somewhat.

In 1988, approximately 700 schools offered graduate business programs. These programs included the traditional two- or three-year graduate programs, four- and five-year evening programs, and two-year "executive" programs designed for the midlevel manager who wants to expand his or her knowledge. Indeed, almost half of those attending MBA programs currently are employed. There is also a general trend toward learning outside the classroom for MBA candidates.

The curriculum found in MBA programs varies, with some emphasizing employee management and others stressing finance and statistical analysis. A typical program might include quantitative analysis, behavioral foundations of management, financial accounting, marketing, economics, human resources, and management of organizational change.

INTERNATIONAL BUSINESS STUDIES

Some colleges are meeting the demand for preparation in international business through certificate programs because few of them have departments of international education. Such a certificate program might include:

1. Requirements for a B.S. or a B.A. in business administration
2. Mathematics in business applications abroad
3. Elements of statistical methods for the metric system
4. Two years of a foreign language
5. Principles of economics, international economics, and comparative economic systems
6. Psychology, sociology, anthropology, geography, history, and political science

International business certificate students are encouraged to spend one or more summers overseas, working or in an exchange program. If you are interested in study abroad, you should request information early from your department head or faculty advisor, to be sure that you have time to meet all course requirements. You may also qualify for assistance for the trip.

Among business schools currently offering exchange curricula for students are New York University and Washington State University. The Programme International de Management is a network of U.S. universities and institutions in West Germany, the United Kingdom, Japan, Sweden, Brazil, Spain, Italy, and Canada. The network offers exchange programs for master's degree business students.

According to *Multinational Business* (Winter, 1989), a primary barrier to the internationalization of U.S. business schools is the limited experience of business school faculty in the international arena. A 1984 survey revealed that only 17 percent of that year's business doctoral students had taken even one course on international business.

Some U.S. universities are beginning to establish business programs in foreign countries. For example, the Amos Tuck School of Business at Dartmouth has opened Japan's first MBA program, and the University of Tennessee is helping to start an MBA program at Karl Marx University.

CORPORATE CLASSROOMS

There is a trend for U.S. corporations to bring education to the workplace and provide their own settings, some of which are quite elaborate. This has become vital at a time when 20 percent of the work force is functionally illiterate. Admittedly, education, when sponsored by a corporation, is for profit rather than for life preparation as when administered by colleges and universities.

However, corporate education is essential to U.S. economic health because by the year 2000, 65 percent of all jobs will require at least a high school education.

American business is spending about $30 billion a year on training. It is estimated that U.S. companies are currently training and educating nearly 11 million people annually, which is close to the total enrollment in America's four-year colleges and universities. Still, the Bureau of Labor Statistics estimates that only 11 percent of employees receive formal job training, and only another 14 percent receive informal training.

Employee-students who attend company schools usually get the courses free of tuition, and some get a full salary while learning.

Universities tend to lag several years behind what is happening in the workplace, whereas the corporate educational system focuses its content on the realities of the business world. Corporate programs are gaining recognition from the same regional accrediting associations that endorse conventional college courses. Classes are taught by company instructors, and some of the programs grant degrees.

Many corporations, especially larger ones, have made major commitments to providing general and technical training for all employees. In suburban Chicago, Motorola has instituted a far-reaching goal of providing forty hours of training a year to every one of its several hundred employees. The "Motorola University" has general curriculum goals, developed by a central staff made up of educators, former executives, and a variety of contract employees. Within that framework, Motorola gives individual company divisions freedom to develop or purchase training geared to their own specific needs.

At Xerox Corporation, management training for newly hired managers (most of whom have MBAs), and for employees moving up the ranks, consists of several phases. The first section, made up of readings and lecture/group participation sessions, is designed to teach employees Xerox's basic principles of service and customer responsiveness.

Subsequent topics include core management skills in finance, personnel, planning, and more. These courses, which last 40 to 60 hours, are taught by company executives and corporate training personnel. To permit students to improve performance in weak areas and to learn new skills, Xerox also offers self-instructional modules for individual study.

Several firms have built their own schools in landscaped settings with golf courses, swimming pools, elaborate teaching/learning equipment, and special living/learning modules with round tables where students can interact. At AT&T's center near Denver, students participate in volleyball games designed to break down communication barriers. Xerox Corporation's setting is a pyramid-type structure in the Virginia woods, while Armstrong World Industries (floor-coverings) meets in a modest nineteenth-century farmhouse outside Lancaster, Pennsylvania. Beneficial Corporation (household finance) has its executives meet on an estate in rural New Jersey. Sun Company uses a mansion near Philadelphia to which they have added classrooms.

These corporate investments are viewed as important tools for teaching corporate culture and style as well as developing management competence. IBM's newest center at Armonk, New York, was especially designed to look important and to demonstrate the company's interest in leadership.

PURSUIT OF EXCELLENCE

A strong trend throughout the United States is to improve the educational system and to search for outstanding individuals. Studies have been made at various levels and areas of specialization. Thomas J. Peters and Robert H. Waterman Jr., together with a group of scholarly business observers, did an in-depth study of

21 American companies.* In order to qualify for the study, a company had to be in the top half of its industry. The researchers identified eight characteristics as contributing to the excellent performance of these companies:

1. They acted. When they had a problem, they got at it immediately. They had reputations for innovation and research.
2. They listened—to customers and employees.
3. They believed that productivity is generated through people.
4. They encouraged experimentation and innovation among their employees and tolerated a reasonable number of failures.
5. Most of their top-level managers came up through the ranks and had hands-on experience.
6. Their organizational structure was lean. They worked hard to keep things simple in a complex world.
7. They had not tried to grow by acquiring companies from unrelated industries.
8. Their management style was simultaneously loose and light—flexible.

Vocationalism

The characteristics of excellence identified by Peters and Waterman reflect another study made of business education a good many years ago.** In that study, schools of business were criticized for two things:

---

*Peters, Thomas J. and Robert H. Waterman, Jr. *In Search of Excellence.* New York: Warner Books, Inc., 1984.
**The Education of American Businessmen.* New York: McGraw-Hill Book Co., 1959.

1. Narrow interpretations (vocationalism) with emphasis on business routines rather than on how to meet business needs for imaginative, flexible, and creative managers.
2. Overemphasis on training for specific jobs, which blocked intellectual growth. This was thought to be especially true of business education for women which encouraged them to prepare for office work.

"Integrity in the College Curriculum: A Report to the Academic Community," is a 1984 report that is also sharply critical of narrow training in some technical and professional areas. It recommends required courses to develop critical thinking, writing, and communication skills, numerical understanding, and historical perspective. It emphasizes the need for a liberal education that teaches ways of understanding and communicating that provide one with access to the world in which we live.

Executives who have received illiterate memos or illogical reports support these recommendations. They recommend in-depth study, value systems, science, international studies, logic and basic reasoning, and communication skills. Executives suggest that students be provided with educational experiences that result in nine basic skills:

1. The ability to think abstractly and perform critical analysis
2. Literacy in writing, reading, speaking, and listening
3. Understanding of numerical data
4. Historical awareness
5. Intellectual ease with science
6. Values and the capacity to make informed moral choices
7. Appreciation of the arts
8. International and multicultural experiences
9. Experience of the personal joy that comes from in-depth study

Studies by the National Institute of Education ("Involvement in Learning") and by William J. Bennett ("To Reclaim a Legacy") both decry the present tendency of college students to take narrow, vocational courses, which are too specifically job oriented. The National Institute of Education urges all students to take at least two full years of liberal arts courses, even if it takes them an extra year to get their degree.

AMERICAN ASSEMBLY OF COLLEGIATE SCHOOLS OF BUSINESS (AACSB)

Colleges and universities that are members of the AACSB have satisfied the standards of accreditation. The AACSB sets standards for admission of students, objectives of the school, curricula, library, finance, educational innovation, and technology. The AACSB requires a "common body of knowledge" in business which includes:

1. Understanding of concepts and processes involved in the production and marketing of goods and/or services and of the financing of a business enterprise.
2. A background in economics and law as they pertain to profit and/or nonprofit organizations, along with an understanding of ethical considerations and social and political influences as they affect such organizations.
3. A basic understanding of concepts and applications of accounting, quantitative methods, and information systems.
4. A study of organization theory, behavior, and interpersonal communications.
5. A study of administrative processes under conditions of uncertainty including integrating analysis and policy determination of the overall management level.

What does AACSB accreditation mean for the person who is selecting a school of business administration? It means that, if accredited, the school meets certain recognized standards. For example, the AACSB takes the position that 40 to 60 percent of the total hours required for a BBA (bachelor of business administration) must be in subjects other than business and economics.

Business students should study nonbusiness electives because courses in physics, biology, or chemistry will help them understand the physical environment in which industries operate. Civics, law, psychology, economics, history, and anthropology help students understand the social environment. Psychology, sociology, administrative processes, and organizational behavior (motivation and group dynamics) supply a base for understanding employees and other personnel. More study in supporting disciplines such as mathematics, logic, and philosophy is also recommended.

A Typical Program

A baccalaureate program may involve 120 semester hours or 186 quarter hours, depending on whether the term is ten or fifteen weeks long. Such a program results in a bachelor's degree in arts, science, or some other special area. Requirements for graduation are specified in a college catalog and may include English composition, health, and physical education, science, math, or history. The following is a typical undergraduate business curriculum:

General Education   *Semester Hrs.*

1. Humanities and fine arts (including English, ...24–27
   language, and literature)

2. Natural science and mathematics (including......................12–24
   calculus and finite math)

3. Behavioral–Social sciences (including................................24
   elementary economics)

   Total general education component..............................60–75

Business Studies

1. Fundamental computer concepts, introduction to financial data, finance management, introduction to financial accounting, computer-based business systems, systems and operations analysis, and financial analysis for managerial decision making

2. Management accounting systems, fundamentals of management, production and operations systems

3. Business communications, business environment, and business policies

4. Marketing concepts

Total business studies component...........................48–54 hrs.

Recommended Electives

Mathematics in business applications, elements of statistical methods, principles of economics, psychology, sociology, or anthropology.

Total elective component ....15–21 hrs.

A minimum CPA (credit point average) of 2.5 is usually required for continued registration and for graduation. (A = 4, B = 3, C = 2, and D = 1) Failure to maintain a 2.5 cumulative CPA automatically puts the student on probation. Students who want to specialize during their undergraduate program may select an option in a department; for example, marketing, accounting, or computer systems.

A trend in business administration emphasizes computer and quantitative math aspects through such courses as discrete mathematics, data structures, algorithmic languages and compiler design, numerical calculus, data base systems, introduction to the theory of computation, and symbolic language programming. More general computer-based courses are management information systems and information systems technology.

EXPERIENCE

Experience is an actual living through of events. It affects judgment, skill, and knowledge; facts and events are observed firsthand rather than related by others. Experience results when you are personally responsible for getting something done—you meet a deadline, finish a task, or earn money. A sense of responsibility and confidence originate from business experience. As a result, you become more employable—more dependable.

Experience should be an integral part of your education. The problem is how to get it. How should you select business experience—or any experience—so that it supplements your education?

Business recruiters who periodically visit campuses to interview potential management candidates express amazement that there are college graduates who apply for jobs with no previous work experience. And, of course, this is unfortunate because organizations will take recruits to train, but they are understandably reluctant to employ one who has not even had a chance to observe what is out there. There are a variety of ways to gain experience, including part-time work and internships.

Part-Time Work

Part-time work can provide valuable business experience, but it does require a commitment. How you handle part-time work while you are in school depends on your other priorities. Some students are able to balance homework, social activities, and a part-time job; others find that either their academic work, their social life, or their job performance begins to suffer. If you would rather not work while going to school, work during the summers, or take a semester or a year off to gain experience that will help you land your first job.

Internships

Internships and cooperative education programs are provided by some schools. An internship may be an extended period away from campus spent on a job—a quarter, a semester, or a year. A cooperative education program is more like a part-time job. Occasionally business organizations sponsor students who live in foreign countries and work there for a semester or a year; students learn the methods and techniques used by specific businesses abroad. Student exchange programs sometimes offer students a chance to work—either in the sponsoring family's business or in the community. All types of experience are helpful.

EDUCATIONAL COSTS

Education is expensive. Tuitions at state universities have risen, as have those at private colleges and universities. To prepare for a management career, a person should plan on completing a baccalaureate degree, which can cost from $4,000 to $15,000 a year, depending on whether one lives at home and whether the school is state supported or private.

According to the U.S. Department of Labor, Bureau of Labor Statistics, managers have more schooling (61.2 percent hold college degrees) than workers in all occupations combined (only 26.4 percent hold college degrees). The proportion of managers with four or more years of college has increased dramatically.

It is also true that there is considerable variation among managers in specific occupations. Self-employed managers who work in small stores have relatively little formal education; more than half have only a high school education or less. However, in technical fields such as data processing and engineering, a graduate degree in business management is helpful. Graduates with an MBA from a prestigious school have an opportunity to move up the management hierarchy in a wide range of industries. Continuing education is also important during a management career.

More information about training programs and career development is available from:

1. American Management Association's Management Information Services (for high school students) or Society for the Advancement of Management (for college students and graduates), 135 West 50th Street, New York, New York 10021
2. International Management Council, 430 S. 20th Street, Omaha, Nebraska 68102

For information about institutions offering special programs in business and management, consult directories or catalogs of institutions of higher learning available in public libraries.

The *Dictionary of Occupational Titles,* (U.S. Department of Labor) also gives a wide range of occupational information. The publication is available in most public libraries.

CHAPTER 5

GETTING PROMOTIONS

How does one measure the success or promotability of a manager? One measure is how effectively the unit being managed gets results, but there are other specific evaluative criteria that change. Supervisory ratings, for example, are not dependable because of personal biases.

The evaluation and promotion of managers is a subjective art. Sometimes getting promoted depends on having the right friends and relatives. At least, it helps when seeking promotions, to have the right connections, provided you also have the ability to lead and get results. Some managers do; and some do not. Some rise from management's base line—supervision—and get on the fast track, climb steadily to the top, and bypass older and more experienced managers. How do they do it? There is no clear-cut answer to the question. More times than not, good guys win, but sometimes they fail. What we look at in this chapter are characteristics of successful managers, tactics some have used, and pitfalls which some managers identify.

GENERALIST VERSUS SPECIALIST

Organizations need professional managers with a flair for getting results, generating enthusiasm, and inspiring confidence. They need innovative managers to shape the organization's future. Business leaders often ask whether this type of direction can best be provided by a generalist or a specialist. Can the broad outlook needed be acquired in a technical area such as accounting or computer science, or through a more general expertise in organizational theory, principles of management, history, and sociology?

People with a specialty get hired for their first job more easily than generalists. When firms recruit, they usually look for someone who can do a particular job such as marketing, accounting, or sales, but sometimes these specially trained employees get stuck in their area of specialization for their entire careers. They become irrevocably identified with their specialty. This tendency is unfortunate because upper management positions demand a broader perspective.

Conclusion No. 1.

Use a specialization to get a job (to get your foot in the door), but start soon thereafter to acquire a broad company outlook. Prepare yourself to speak, think, and act in terms of a broad company overview.

FRIENDS, MENTORS, SPONSORS

Everyone needs friends, mentors, and sponsors to speak for them and to use as a sounding board. Possibly, one can rise in an organization on individual merit alone, but it is nicer and easier to have a helping hand reach out along the way.

In most organizations, the politics of who gets what, from whom (and for what) is important. Organizations are usually dominated by an in-group which sets priorities, and those who succeed easily are the ones who achieve sponsorship from members of the in-group.

A sponsor—preferably from higher up in the organization— should vouch for and defend you in higher company circles. In firms that promote strictly from within, sponsorship is an absolute requirement for getting ahead.

The word *sponsor* is defined as one who accepts responsibility for another. Sponsors of young managers speak for them; they recommend them for promotions and programs but do not assure satisfactory results. Sponsors help new managers get a chance to show what they can do, but sponsors do not assume specific responsibility for how new managers perform.

Young employees often make the mistake of thinking that they do not need help from older, established members of the company. This is not necessarily overconfidence, but it shows that young employees are unaware of the importance of having sponsors. This is not to suggest that young employees should "butter up" to senior managers. However, it is practical and realistic, especially if you do not have connections in a firm, to find someone who will take an interest in your progress and learn enough about your ability to speak for you in higher places. It is questionable whether one's boss and one's sponsor should be the same person.

Conclusion No. 2.

Those who aspire to climb the precarious ladder of success should cultivate friends a rung or two higher who will extend a helping hand when needed.

Some sponsors are called mentors. A mentor can be a sponsor, but a sponsor is not necessarily a mentor. A mentor gives advice and listens to grievances when the employee needs help. A mentor teaches, counsels, and helps an employee grow on the job. A mentor can also serve as a role model. Sponsors recommend a person; they nominate him or her for projects or committees.

In companies where the practice of ''mentoring'' is encouraged, meetings between neophytes and seasoned managers may be held regularly to review events and discuss plans. These can be monthly, morning coffee sessions or decision-making meetings with trainees invited as observers.

EVALUATIONS

Management evaluation takes many forms and is used to provide information about performance. It is difficult to evaluate employees objectively; favoritism is a problem. Much study has been given to performance reviews. Reviews of young middle managers are particularly important in order to find those who are having personnel problems and who show judgmental weaknesses of various types. If detected early, such flaws can possibly be corrected through counseling or additional training.

Companies that become bankrupt have often said that the real problem was managers who were unable to make good decisions or who made costly misjudgments. For example, a large corporation recently in the news because of bankruptcy, referred to its senior management group as ''reclusive and controversial'' about marketing decisions. This management group apparently lost the confidence of middle management and employees down the line. Shipments were delayed, and retail outlets closed. Company projects and programs faltered, and more alert personnel began to leave the firm.

A classic example of a costly management misjudgment is the Edsel automobile. It was apparently put on the market at the wrong time, and the mistake cost the Ford Motor Company millions of dollars. Most companies cannot survive such costly mistakes.

Unfortunately, it is the stockholders and customers who pay for mismanagement—and the employees who lose their jobs.

The technique of having employees evaluate a manager is probably the poorest method. Most employees will not objectively complete even an unsigned checksheet appraisal of their manager. They may do so privately, but not as part of a study that is likely to get back to the manager.

Some managers look for informal appraisal from good friends outside the company or from their spouses. The obvious problem here is that a spouse or best friend is rarely objective. Other managers turn to psychologists, but they too are at a disadvantage because they get only one side of the picture—the manager's. In a few instances, consulting psychologists have been brought into organizations. Through a series of observed situations, manager performance is evaluated either by a committee or by designated individuals. Training needs are identified and addressed, and then performance is again observed. Junior or middle managers trained in this way may be interviewed by senior managers other than those to whom they report. They may be given plan-making assignments which are reviewed and appraised by experienced managers.

MANAGEMENT FLOW

A relatively new way to judge management performance is by length of service at one level; that is, which employees are stuck on plateaus? Flow of personnel from one category to another as managers advance is desirable. Analysis of the rate of movement, or flow, identifies managers with good potential as well as those who are less likely to advance. For example, management trainees at the junior or middle level who do not move out of the initially assigned category within a reasonable time will probably be shelved or dismissed. Management recruits should make sure they understand how they will be evaluated. What criteria will be used, by whom, and how?

Some people have unrealistic expectations about how far they can move up in an organization or how fast. It takes years for the majority of junior managers to move even to middle management. Quick achievement (promotion), for the majority of managers, is unrealistic.

A management flow analysis of 400 managers showed that 312 stayed in the same category throughout the years, 13 were demoted from middle to junior management, 33 left, and 42 were promoted—22 from junior management to middle, and 20 from middle to top.

Computer Appraisal

If a company uses a computer to calculate management flow, other factors can be introduced: age, sex, ethnicity, length of service, time on present job, education, or percent of merit increase. Managers could also be grouped by function—accounting, marketing, sales—and by levels, department sizes, and size of budget. A cross analysis of this type, made possible by computer capabilities, creates an entirely new base for management appraisal. Other, less specific variables—such as money earned for the corporation by a particular function or strategies developed—could read like a statement of assets on a company's balance sheet. Indeed it is a human resources, or leadership, balance sheet—a new device for monitoring and managing human resources systems.

Conclusion No. 3.

Companies can create a computer data base for management appraisals by calculating flow or movement from one level to another in combination with factors such as age, length of ser-

*vice, education, percent of merit increase, department size, and
size of budget.*

POLITICS AND PATRONAGE

Unsophisticated young recruits fresh from college may think their technical qualifications play the most important part in their advancement, but it is possible that company politics and "seats of power" within the organization are more important—and hard to combat because of prejudices and jealousies.

When a manager is hired, both formal and informal expectations should be clarified. Informal expectations may be even more important than formal or technical ones. For example, the organization's formal image of a promotable executive and their dress code may not agree at all with the new employee's; the general environment may be stressful because of underlying restlessness and poor attitude among employees. There may be a lot of behind-the-scenes complaining.

These possibilities indicate that recruits should be selective about the organization they join. Job candidates need to ask questions such as the following when evaluating a job offer and looking for a career path with a company:

1. Is the company's "personality" compatible with mine?
2. What is the overall company climate?
3. Are management's attitudes progressive?
4. Who handles promotions?
5. How are employees identified for promotion?
6. Is the company community oriented?
7. Will I be expected to take part in community (civic) projects?
8. What are the pressure periods in this company?
9. How much overtime am I expected to work?

CASE STUDIES

The following case studies were taken from *The Corporate Promotables** and illustrate some pitfalls that may await aspiring management recruits:

Insubordination

I used to be plant manager at our Texas facility and had been there about four years. This plant has always been sort of a stepchild due to the necessity for its location. Maintenance expenses on the production facilities and capital retirements have always been much higher than for the other plants . . . . Of course, this can't be prevented . . . which everybody recognizes.

I was doing quite well with production higher than the previous plant managers and had maintenance and retirements down a little. Then we got a new general manager, and he started pushing for maintenance control. I tried to tell him you couldn't improve much and so did some others, what with the salt water all the hell over everything, but he wouldn't listen.

Finally, I got frustrated and told him I was doing as well or better than anyone else and if he thought he could do better why didn't he run it himself. I was sore.

Well, that did it, I committed the cardinal crime—insubordination. Two weeks later I was here, and I've been here ever since. My career is ended. He just won't tolerate any back talk. I found out the hard way. This happened almost five years ago, and I'm too old to go with another company. That's all there is to it.

---

*Adams, Sexton. and Don Fyffe. *The Corporate Promotables*.
Houston Gulf Publishing Co., 1969, 86–94. Used with permission.

Apple Polishing

I used to work for another electronics firm, and they really pushed for production, which was OK with me. I can work as hard as the next guy.

My line produced as much as any of the others and more than most. You won't believe this, but upper management expected you to come in on Sundays, too, not to work, but just to be seen on the premises—supposed to show how much you loved the darn place.

Well, I have a family. What are you supposed to do, live at the plant? Lots of the foremen came down to the lounge on Sunday and drank coffee for a couple of hours. I did a few times, then said to hell with it—it's not worth it. It would make more sense if you worked at something. But just being seen, why it's plain ridiculous.

I started to get passed over for promotions, and I finally asked why. My boss said they weren't sure about my attitude and for me to think about it. Attitude! How does that grab you? So I quit and came here.

Do It Right

All right, so maybe I'm stupid. But I've been taught all my life if something is worth doing, it is worth doing well—and that's my problem.

We have some of the most outdated procedures you can imagine, and periodically we get instructions which just make things worse. I don't think it's right to just sit back and take it. What kind of men are we anyway? So I buck the system, try to point out the improvements we can and should make.

You know what that makes me? A troublemaker. I have the reputation up the line for being a troublemaker. But the other supervisors all agree we aren't operating properly, so it's not just me. They always want me to take exception to things and try to get things corrected. They must figure I'm dead anyway and they're right. I'm not going any place with this company.

The Young Obsoletes

When we began to grow rapidly, I automatically assumed my chances for promotion would be greatly increased. They weren't. The company figures you have to move the men so fast to get them to the upper levels of management that those of us who are experienced are expected to run the business while we train the kids to be our bosses. I'm 38 and have 27 years to go with the company, but suddenly I'm too old. One of my friends is too old at 31 to progress in his department. The age limit is 28.

I'm interested in this company . . . but I'd be better off personally if we didn't have so many openings. When things are tougher economically, they have to promote the capable people, the ones who can produce now. It may sound ridiculous, but a mild recession with retarded growth would make me promotable again. I can't believe the whole situation is completely rational.

Conclusion No. 4.

Be selective about the firm you join. Try to see behind the scenes. Is it a place where you really want to work?

KEYS TO PROMOTION

The preceding stories give only one person's point of view—the manager's. What kind of people were these managers? What were their attitudes and personal relations skills? Often the fault is not in the situation but in ourselves. Studies of successful executives stress different characteristics. For example, some attribute success to flexibility of management style, breadth of knowledge about the organization, hard work, or ability to bring plans to satisfactory completion. Others say it is who you know.

The need to achieve results is of the essence in management at any level. Logically, it seems there is only one qualification for promotability: performance. Yet, two sets of factors need to be examined: (1) personal characteristics and (2) learned, or acquired, characteristics. Recruiters view certain characteristics as signs of promising management potential.

Personal Characteristics

Personal characteristics indicative of a manager with good potential include the following:

1. Needs to excel, is energetic, has drive
2. Seeks challenging opportunities
3. Takes risks willingly
4. Assumes responsibilities courageously
5. Thinks creatively, gets new ideas and understands new ideas of others
6. Admits mistakes, is flexible
7. Thinks in terms of *why;* likes to know reasons behind things
8. Likes to think ahead of others and be in the lead
9. Negotiates easily and willingly
10. Knows how to get around at work—politically and socially
11. Keeps up-to-date about new management practicums
12. Seeks leadership experiences
13. Works easily with a variety of people
14. Has a certain charisma or flair
15. Is results oriented and a positive thinker
16. Has a sense of humor

Acquired Skills

1. Self-discipline
2. Time management
3. Delegation
4. Patience: tolerance and human understanding, fairness
5. Self-confidence
6. Ability to get at facts and make decisions
7. Ability to implement plans
8. Concentration and perseverance
9. Ability to think quantitatively
10. Ability to work with associates
11. Communication skills
12. Ability to evaluate possible employees
13. Ability to be a cooperative team worker
14. Ability to handle stress and conflict
15. Ability to balance personal and business life

Performance Versus Personality

Out of 56 possible factors influencing promotion, managers selected the following as very helpful:

Argues logically
Works with a minimum of direction
Has a record of accomplishments
Has the respect of associates
Comes up with new ways to handle problems
Has a sponsor at a higher level
Can motivate and develop subordinates
Communicates effectively, listens well
Meets deadlines
Can sell ideas
Is tactful

Understands the emotional make-up of people
Is willing to move geographically, change location

In addition to these performance skills, the following personality characteristics were rated as somewhat helpful:

Accepts criticism and admits mistakes
Goes by the book
Looks and behaves like a manager, good appearance
Bends the rules to get things done, knows when to make
　exceptions
Is active in the community
Is ambitious, has a career strategy
Does not complain
Takes suggestions from subordinates
Is willing to work more than 40 hours a week
Expresses disagreement diplomatically

Common deficiencies among managers are, for the most part, the reverse of the personality characteristics just listed. For example:

Wastes time
Has no drive
Avoids taking risks
Procrastinates
Communicates awkwardly
Puts the wrong people on task forces
Projects a poor authority image, does not evoke respect
Plans ineffectively
Obsessed with details
Is too complacent; hence, department no longer dynamic

CONCLUSION

A variety of personality and performance factors are considered when appraising managers for promotion. Executives are carefully developed as a precious company resource, and companies constantly watch junior and middle management levels for new talent. Many standard factors influence the success of managers, but there are always exceptions. Some mavericks disregard the suggestions in this chapter and proceed in their own way, even though too much nonconformity is not recommended for those coming up in the ranks.

If the expectations described in this chapter are unacceptable to you, then you have two alternatives: find an organization with a more compatible philosophy or change your aspirations and decide to stay put. Perhaps the organization is too big or too small for you. Smaller companies provide a wide range of opportunities and freedom of action. Working for a family-owned business—unless it is your own—may, however, be restrictive. Before you decide you cannot tolerate appraisal patterns of large corporations, be sure your expectations are realistic.

Whatever style of organization you prefer, you will want to make a commitment that will give you and your employer satisfaction and provide a basis for mutual growth. It does you no good to work within an organization whose goals, needs, and demands go against your own values or strong beliefs. Selecting the company carefully, and then making a full, whole-hearted commitment is basic to your career development. Having a career plan of your own will help you to do this. Once you have examined and planned for your own career goals, you will be more realistic in choosing the company you want to join, or in building your own company to further your goals.

CHAPTER 6

SUCCESS AND BENEFITS

Are you becoming the kind of person you want to be?
Are you doing the things you want to do?
Are you reaching your goals?

If you can say ''yes'' to these questions, consider yourself successful—at least for the time being, because success is relative. It changes with time and conditions. For example, adults and teenagers have different goals for success.

Success has different meanings. What one person considers as a successful achievement (for example, running a mile in four minutes or spending a day without arguing with the children) may be pointless to another. The meaning of success depends on your value system and expectations, personality, drive, education, health, and maturity, and, of course—timing.

Most people, particularly businesspeople, may associate success primarily with wealth and social status. For others, it may mean mastery of an art, science, or trade, and the development of outstanding work, or it can mean the development of good human relationships in creating and maintaining a home. For young people just starting a career, success may mean having landed the type of job they want in a firm they like. In the latter situation, further success will be associated with learning the job, improving work performance, dealing with workday problems, getting along

69

with co-workers, gaining visibility in the office, or being recognized as an achiever.

CHARACTERISTICS OF SUCCESS

Success does not just happen. It usually results from being positive enough to achieve a desired goal. It may start with a very small achievement which leads to others; small successes are the foundation of bigger ones.

A success-oriented attitude is essential. Show pride in your position, in the company, and in the product or service it renders. Be a company person. Dress for a management leadership role, and project an aura of competence and confidence. If you have a poor attitude and do not care, no one else is likely to care either.

Modern managers operate in a high-pressure environment. The pressures of the job increase as managers strive to function within the economic, legal, and social limits of their market environment. Some pressures are generated by the personalities of the managers themselves: drive to achieve, to gain ego satisfaction and social status.

Achievement provides self-confidence and the inspiration and energy to go after new goals. Few individuals possess the entire range of characteristics attributed to great leaders. If you are lucky enough to possess one or two characteristics of strength, develop them.

To be successful, you must care enough to make the big effort. Start by making a list of success factors, set some goals, and monitor your progress. Accumulate a few guidelines that are especially meaningful to you. Refer to your guidelines often.

Some characteristics of success are as follows:

Optimism	Respect for others
Interest	Courtesy

Industry	Loyalty
Creativity	Integrity
Friendliness	

What do these characteristics mean to you? Are they just words? Write definitions of them on three-by-five cards to carry in a pocket, or tape to a mirror at home, and review them from time to time.

Optimism. It is easy to be optimistic; optimism is a point of view. Merely take a positive rather than a negative point of view when you meet unfamiliar situations. Optimism is contagious. It spreads from you to others and, given other factors such as ability and knowledge, it helps you reach career goals more easily. It is better to be optimistic than to always shake your head ''no'' and say, ''We tried that once before, and it didn't work.''

Interest. How can you be successful if you are not interested in the work or the company? Interest is an attitude; to become interested, learn all you can about your job. Understand how your work relates to that of co-workers; find out what procedures they use. Learn about the company; read company manuals. Ask questions when you do not understand a situation. Why feel embarrassed about asking for explanations? Would you rather learn after the work is done incorrectly?

When you ask questions about your work and company, you take the first step toward creating a successful environment for yourself. Try wording job-related questions as follows:

- Can you give me more detail about that point so that I understand it better?
- Can you give me an example of what you mean?
- Would you repeat what you just said so that I can get it straight?
- May I repeat to you in my own words what I think I heard you say? I want to be sure that I understand.

- Could I try that while you watch to be sure I really understand what you have been showing me?

Ask questions, yes—but ask meaningful ones. It is important to know what kind of questions to ask, where to ask them, and how to recognize when you have asked too many. When you ask unnecessary questions, unrelated to the situation at hand, or questions whose answers are easily found elsewhere, you plant seeds of doubt about your ability. Therefore, think about the questions you ask before you ask them. Are they necessary, or can you get the information elsewhere? Do they relate to the task at hand? Also, when you ask a question, *listen to the answer.* You may want to take notes or ask clarifying questions about the answer given.

Industry. Are you looking for a soft job, or are you willing to work? Real achievers—those who do something beyond the ordinary—are hard workers and usually spend more than the minimum forty hours a week at work. They do more than the minimum and seek out challenging tasks. They volunteer just for the experience. Studies show that people are happiest when working, especially at something they like to do. Willingness to work is a trait that identifies an emotionally stable and well-adjusted person.

When things need to be done, why not get into the act, cooperate, and do them? Willingness to lend a helping hand during pressure periods is noticed by co-workers as well as by supervisors. It wins points for you which, when accumulated, may earn goodwill and promotions. It also helps you grow in job responsibility. Seek new responsibilities; ask for new duties you think you can handle. Willingness to work and to assume new responsibilities mark you as a "comer" and identify you for future successes. Don't wait to be asked; show interest and give that little something extra.

As you assume greater job responsibility, invest your time carefully to achieve your goals. You need not put in overtime or carry work home every day. Instead, learn to concentrate during working hours, avoiding idle chatter and time killers.

Creativity. Creating and implementing new ideas is the essence of progress. Some people are naturally creative and easily find ways of putting their ideas to work in simplifying procedures, developing projects, or weeding out nonessentials. These people are innovators, and managers need this trait, but innovation can be overdone. It is unsettling to work with people who are always changing things. Seeing things in a new light and looking at alternative plans is good, but do not start big changes until you have been on a job for awhile. And when you do start to put your creativity into practice, consider others. Be tactful about how you introduce new ideas. Try not to impose your ideas on others.

Friendliness. Recognize the importance of relating well to people, both on and off the job. To some extent, you are judged by your friends. What type of friends do you have? Are your friends successful, or grumblers and excuse makers—the ones who tear things down? If you seek success in business, associate with success-oriented people. Why not pick friends who are going places instead of chronic complainers?

The enthusiasm of success-oriented people rubs off in several ways. It affects your attitude, which in turn affects the way others work with you. It is surely better to work in a friendly environment than with complainers who try to explain their own shortcomings by blaming others. Be practical; if you want to be a success, find successful friends.

Respect for Others. Some people generate bad personal chemistry and feed their egos by tearing down others. Avoid associating with these people because they invite trouble. Everyone likes to be respected. Successful leaders recognize this need and build team spirit on it.

Treat others with respect. Respect their opinions, their time, workstations and property, their efforts, and their right to speak out, even when they disagree with you. Respect their right to be different from you. If you take a positive attitude toward others, they will treat you likewise.

Courtesy. Courtesy is also based on respect for others and shows itself in many ways. For example, in business, courtesy shows itself in such things as tone of voice, not interrupting, the way you address others, and the way you react to what they say. Discourtesy (rudeness) often results from impatience and irritation when things are not going right. Unfortunately, rudeness makes enemies and hurts people's feelings. No one likes to be pushed, interrupted, or treated brusquely. Hurt feelings often never heal.

Loyalty. Do you criticize your company and gossip about its methods or personnel? If a company has enough confidence in your ability to hire you, you owe the company and its other employees loyalty. If you cannot be loyal, find another job. Otherwise, in time, you will acquire a negative personality which will make you a tiresome person and detract from your career opportunities.

Working in an environment where you cannot feel loyal will ultimately destroy you. You may not agree with everything the company or your associates do, but then, you may not have all the facts either. So be fair. Do not overreact to situations and rumors when you have only secondhand or partial information. Keep an open mind, and have confidence in the judgment and ability of your co-workers. Be loyal to them. It is a good idea to learn what you can about your boss, the boss's boss, and your co-workers so that you can better understand how to work with them.

Integrity. If you try to be honest, patient, and fair with associates, they learn to trust you, and that will bring out the best in them when they work with you. Subordinates must be able to depend on their leaders, or the whole organization will fall apart. A sense of trust among co-workers creates a climate of confidence and harmony. A reputation for fairness, dependability, and honesty must be earned, but once achieved, it can be one of your best assets when you are evaluated for promotion or assigned new responsibilities. Integrity provides a firm foothold from which to climb in an organization.

Other attributes of successful managers are ambition, adaptability, ability to communicate, ability to organize, decisiveness, and personal dynamism.

Many of us have known successful managers who were impatient and outrageously demanding managers; individuals who were excessively opinionated, indecisive, unable to delegate, and so forth. On the whole, however, successful managers display the more desirable management attitudes, skills, and characteristics described above.

FAILURE

One thing that worries many of us is failure. Many of us also fret about not being accepted by our peers. These problems can be best overcome through education, experience, and self-confidence. Confidence can be built through expertise and success on the job. Success breeds respect and self-satisfaction, as well as more success. Assume an "I get results" attitude. Once you acquire a reputation among your peers for being able to get good results without flak and tension, you are on your way.

Success sometimes depends on seemingly trivial things. Again and again, we are reminded in career development literature that people often fail because they cannot get along with others. Think about that. The most frequent cause of on-the-job failure is when people do not want to work with you, or when you cannot work harmoniously with them.

People may not work well with others who are troublemakers. Troublemakers, by habit or because of temporary frustration, may make sharp or upsetting remarks about others or the work at hand.

They may be slow to cooperate, take negative points of view, or complain and spread rumors. They may ask prying, personal questions.

These habits can upset an organization's entire staff and cause a great deal of trouble. If you find yourself developing any of these habits, try to analyze the cause and take care of the problem. If you cannot handle the problem yourself, perhaps counseling will help. It's well worthwhile to keep yourself from allowing a negative pattern to become entrenched.

DELEGATION

Delegation is a way for managers to multiply their effectiveness while training and developing employees. When delegated, tasks are assigned to employees to be performed either under supervision or through report-back accountability. Successful managers know how to delegate; they are judged, in part, by their ability to develop subordinates. After all, it is management's responsibility to get work done through others.

Some managers, especially at operative levels, are afraid to delegate because they think the work won't be done right—it won't be done their way. Some managers also dislike releasing any of their power or authority. In today's complex organizations, however, it is essential that managers delegate for two reasons: (1) to develop subordinates and (2) to allow for company growth. If managers cannot delegate, their capacity to handle additional work is severely limited.

Delegating does not mean simply handing something to an employee and saying, "Have this ready for me tomorrow." Good managers discuss how and when the employee should report progress; they set goals and clarify instructions. Training may be necessary—depending on what is being delegated. Once a task is delegated, managerial snooping is not recommended.

Good delegation is assigning a project to someone else and trusting that person to do it right. It is a sure way to involve employees in goal-setting and planning, because they must know not only what, but why, when, with what resources, by whom, and according to what priority. It is important for a manager and subordinate to agree on standards for measuring results, including deadlines and minimum quality of work.

If an employee is not doing well, the assignment should not be snatched away unless the problem is very serious. Making mistakes is a valuable learning experience, and everyone makes them. If a manager snatches back a task because an employee makes a mistake, that employee's initiative and morale will surely be damaged. It is better to give the employee more instruction, examples, and an opportunity to complete the job well. Once an assignment is satisfactorily finished, the manager should express his or her approval.

Delegation Checklist*

When to Delegate:

- When someone else can do it as well as you or better.
- When you might do it poorly because of lack of time.
- When subordinates can do it well enough for the cost or time involved.
- When a subordinate can't do it as well but your doing it interferes with something more important. Delegate, coach the subordinate on how to do it, and expect less satisfactory

---

*Reprinted, by permission of the publisher, from *Mastering Assertiveness Skills* by Elaina Zuker © 1983 Elaina Zuker. Published by AMACOM, a division of American Management Associations, 135 West 50th Street, New York, NY 10020. All rights reserved.

results than you would achieve. If this can't be done, subordinates may be unqualified to do this job. You need controls on this situation.

- When a project will be useful for developing a subordinate, if costs or time permit, and if you can afford the risk.
- When it actually costs too much for you to do it.
- When you are spending too much of your time on operations.

When Not to Delegate:

- When no one can do it as well as you and when the time it will take you isn't out of proportion with its importance.
- When it's confidential or beyond what subordinates can handle.
- When it doesn't cost too much for you to do it, or when the time of passing it on would consume the savings.
- When you have to set the pace and pattern, to show how to take long steps.
- When you must keep close enough to see trends, keep informed, maintain control, and so on. If delegating keeps you too far from certain matters that you must be informed on, then the question is not, ''Can the employee do it?'' but rather ''Can I keep necessary control by delegating?''

EXPERIENCE

Successful management skills are developed best through a variety of firsthand experiences rather than through secondhand activities such as reading, talking, or writing. For example, describing the parts of a rifle will not teach a soldier to use it; lecturing to students about the theory of internal combustion will not make them good auto mechanics. The same holds true for management skills. If you want to be an effective manager, you must learn through hands-on experience.

Obviously, not everyone is interested in a management career. Finding and motivating those who are takes time. New managers need a receptive and positive attitude toward the learning process. Recruits need to seek a broad base of experience and meet and work with a wide variety of people, some of whom may reject or disparage them.

There is no substitute for the right experience. Those who study successful executives observe that these managers have skills that are not learned in formal educational programs, even in graduate school. They are skilled at assessing and leading people; getting along with others and knowing how to make their subordinates feel good about working with them.

Good managers take personal responsibility for getting things done and accept the consequences of their actions. They also learn from feedback about their activities.

How do aspiring managers get the kind of experience they need? The seriously career-oriented person finds ways to combine academic training with opportunities to learn by doing—in school, in church, and in community-related extracurricular activities such as sports and scout work.

> The *do* is essential to learning. Lectures, case discussions, or textbooks alone are of limited value in developing ability to find opportunities and problems. Guided practice in finding them in real business situations is the only method that will make a manager skillful in identifying the right things to do. . . .*

---

*Livingston, Sterling. "Myth of the Well-Educated Manager." *Harvard Business Review* (January/February 1971): 84.

GUIDELINES

As you begin your management career, the following guidelines collected from the experiences of others may help to point the way. Try to apply them and make them work for you.

1. Hours of learning lead to years of achievement.
2. Equip yourself for a leadership role. Knowledge and techniques of management will help you be a better manager than someone who is not professionally qualified. Managers continue to need career education to keep up with new trends.
3. Managers are paid for achievement, not for personality. Learn to evaluate your results.
4. Pause periodically to take inventory: Where are you going with your career? Which of yesterday's goals have you met? Where do you want to go next?
5. What changes do you want to make in yourself? Think about your personal philosophy, self-discipline, interpersonal relations, and education in relation to the cultural environment in which you live.
6. The only way to become equal is to feel equal. Do you wear your anxieties on your sleeve?
7. Do not undervalue the contributions you can make. If you were not important to the company, you would not be there. Evaluate your contributions realistically; then decide to upgrade them.
8. In settling conflicts, keep your remarks brief and as impersonal as possible. Whether the other persons involved are furious or just concerned, the guideline is the same. Keep your cool, and hear them out. Concentrate on listening.
9. Become a skillful change maker. Learn how to introduce and implement change. Prepare yourself and your associates for coming changes. Create and introduce gradually the setting which includes your changes.

10. Discipline yourself to make personal and social commitments needed for success in leadership. It takes an investment of time, money, self, and work to succeed. Are you ready to make this investment?

No one can offer an exact formula for success in business management. There is no list of "five easy steps" to help you reach the top. You will need intelligence, will, and character. You can probably make it if you take time to reaffirm personal values, stay in control of yourself, and learn to manage the forces of change that affect you.

CHAPTER 7

THE MANAGEMENT TOOLBOX

Surviving as a successful manager requires more than just the ability to operate a computer or analyze product costs. To survive in the high-pressure world of business, prospective managers must prepare themselves to cope with the change, stress, and human interaction that are such large parts of management. By learning skills for handling the emotional aspects of management, the beginning manager can help assure a long, happy career.

This chapter explains ways to improve human relations with others in the workplace, how to maintain good physical and mental conditions on the job, and how to remain challenged by your work.

REMAINING CHALLENGED

Everything changes; people age, technology advances, and companies grow and fail. Whether a manager remains at one company for years or changes jobs frequently, he or she needs to remain aware of changes in business methods. The use of personal computers is a prime example of this need to respond to new realities.

Before the advent of the personal computer, the executive had a secretary who typed letters. If an executive wanted to review a report, it was prepared and brought in by a subordinate. If changes were needed, the subordinate left and returned with the changes the manager requested.

However, the advent of the personal computer in the 1980s shifted much of the responsibility for creating and manipulating data directly to the manager. Managers who could not type (after all, that was clerical work) suddenly found themselves confronted by a keyboard. Those with no mechanical aptitude found that they were expected to transfer their handwritten operations to a complex machine. For some, the computer was a breakthrough that expanded their ability to manage. For others, it is an object of fear.

Adapting to change and viewing new experiences as positive are vital to avoiding job boredom, skills obsolescence, and performance deterioration. As more is learned about human and procedural deterioration and as we see how they affect people and things, we understand better what must be done to reactivate ourselves.

Here are a few generalizations which may serve as brief guidelines:

1. Some people are more aware of change than others. Some try to retool as needed by acquiring new knowledge, reviewing their goals, and preparing for changes that loom ahead. They try to keep their careers from going to seed.
2. Think about what the future holds for you. Anticipate and plan ahead. Time passes quickly, and unless you do some long-range planning, you may be caught unprepared.
3. An important factor is to keep yourself mentally alert. Open minds open doors to new ideas, new life-styles, new solutions, and new perspectives. Some people associate the inability to change with aging, but people do not need to fall into mental stupors as they age. In order not to do so,

however, they must exercise, eat right, and retain the ability to learn by doing new things, meeting new people, and being with people who try to stay mentally alert.

4. Avoid being lulled by comfortable habits and old attitudes. Life is more fulfilling for those who stay mentally alert by trying new things and staying open to change.

5. Everything you do reflects habits, skills, and attitudes that were years in the making. They are part of your life-style and personal philosophy. A basic problem of self-renewal is to keep from growing stale and living in the past. Everyone has this problem when fighting personal obsolescence. Everyone has the problem of growing "barnacles" derived from family tradition and past experiences.

MATURITY

The dictionary defines maturity as a state of perfect or complete development. To reach such a state is surely a goal of self-renewal because this is the type of maturity we look for in leaders. Maturity means that one has grown up so as to be an asset to the human race. A mature person should be able to handle events at home and at work with the least possible amount of stress.

Maturity is associated with age. People are supposed to be wiser and more sensible as they get older because they have had more experience. Everything ages with time, but it does not necessarily follow that a person is better or wiser merely because of age. The type of maturity looked for in business leaders is a companion to good mental health and not just part of the aging process. Maturity carries with it the capacity to accept courageously disappointments that are beyond our control, to endure illness, to accept ourselves and others with tolerance, and to keep on an even keel—through success as well as failure. This type of maturity develops gradually—through experience and the ability to handle exasperating situations without creating enemies.

Continuing education can help us acquire maturity, but education is only part of the preparation. Everyone faces situations for which education alone does not prepare them. Nor do so-called adult education programs assure maturity, although self-renewal is one object of adult education. Enthusiasm, courage, reliability, humbleness, self-appraisal—all these things and more contribute to maturity.

An early sign of maturity is the ability to meet unexpected situations without falling apart, to "roll with the punches" without looking for someone to blame. Each situation offers opportunities for mature or immature responses. Some of us learn from such opportunities, but others do not.

Maturity is a very important leadership characteristic and should be a self-renewal goal. Those in leadership positions, from presidents of corporations down to line supervisors, must be mature enough to provide the stability which we associate with wholesome leadership. To help others grow is a high-level human relations activity. It takes mature people to lead.

Take the opportunity to learn from those around you in developing role models and assessing your own maturity. There will always be plentiful opportunities to observe others, assess their level of maturity in handling situations, and compare it to your own. An honest appraisal of your behavior in stressful situations will help you to keep track of your development. In a very short time, you will have amassed enough experience to be aware of your own developing maturity. Learning from your own mistakes and from your own growth is a part of developing maturity, and the opportunity is open to all of us, as long as we remain open to change.

STRESS

The inability to adapt to change is a principal cause of stress. Stress among managers may also result from high performance expectations, personal problems, and a variety of other reasons.

A certain amount of stress is expected by anyone who works, and this stress is normal. An employee who is not experiencing some stress probably is not working hard enough. However, excessive stress may harm work productivity and even damage health.

Many organizations are consulting psychologists about the problem and are sponsoring stress seminars for their employees. Some organizations are even being sued by employees who contend that their work was unduly stressful.

Most stress consultants are psychologists. Some are known as psychotherapists. Although Robert Pater is not a psychologist, his advice to managers who are responsible for personnel programs summarizes very well suggestions for coping with the problem within the corporation.

1. *Set up a unified approach to organizational stress management, by providing avenues for listening to and, where possible, correcting, employee concerns.* ''I've found that the distinguishing factor between employees who brood and blame their employer for all of their problems and those who leave gracefully or seek professional help is that the 'claimers' tend to be people of low self-esteem who feel that they were not treated well and not listened to by their employer.''

2. *Decide what types of stress are specific to your organization and what types aren't.* ''Do you have a planned approach to responding to all stress claims? Such an approach should correspond to your sexual harassment and age discrimination policies.''

3. *Get input regarding organizational stress management and claims reduction from all bargaining units, representative employees, top managers, and supervisors.*
4. *Train personnel in stress management skills, including the importance to the bottom line.* Train supervisors how to recognize signs of harmful stress, how it affects productivity and absenteeism, and how to deal with employees suffering from stress. Train employees, too, in stress management skills.
5. *Develop an ongoing support program.* Provide for an employee assistance program; train employees as stress management trainers or peer counselors, "courts of first resort." One-shot training is of minimal use unless it is followed up.
6. *Be more cautious in screening and hiring employees.* Look for a good fit. Sometimes, in a buyer's market, a "good buy"—an overqualified new hire—can be a setup for problems. It's also generally unwise to hire an ambitious, creative person to fill what you know to be a dead-end, repetitive position.*

The following quiz will help you evaluate your current levels of stress.

---

*The Oregonian (April 1985): 12.

Stress Quiz

Answer each question based on your own experience in the past 12 months by placing a check in the appropriate column. To find your score, look on page 90.

	NO	YES
1. Have you lived or worked in a noisy area?	☐	☐
2. Have you changed your living conditions or moved?	☐	☐
3. Have you had trouble with in-laws?	☐	☐
4. Have you taken out a large loan or mortgage?	☐	☐
5. Have you tended to fall behind with the things you should do?	☐	☐
6. Have you found it difficult to concentrate at times?	☐	☐
7. Have you frequently had trouble going to sleep?	☐	☐
8. Have you found that you tend to eat, drink, or smoke more than you really should?	☐	☐
9. Have you watched more than three hours of television daily for weeks at a time?	☐	☐
10. Have you or your spouse changed jobs or work responsibilities?	☐	☐
11. Have you been dissatisfied or unhappy with your work or felt excessive work responsibilities?	☐	☐
12. Has a close friend died?	☐	☐
13. Have you been dissatisfied with your sex life?	☐	☐
14. Have you been pregnant?	☐	☐
15. Have you had an addition to the family?	☐	☐
16. Have you worried about making ends meet?	☐	☐
17. Has one of the family had bad health?	☐	☐
18. Have you taken tranquilizers from time to time?	☐	☐
19. Have you frequently found yourself becoming easily irritated when things don't go well?	☐	☐
20. Have you often experienced bungled human relations— even with those you love most?	☐	☐
21. Have you found that you are often impatient or edgy with your children or other family members?	☐	☐
22. Have you tended to feel restless or nervous much of the time?	☐	☐
23. Have you had frequent headaches or digestive upsets?	☐	☐
24. Have you experienced anxiety or worry for days at a time?	☐	☐
25. Have you often been so preoccupied that you have forgotten where you put things or forgotten whether you have turned off machinery?	☐	☐
26. Have you been married or reconciled with your spouse?	☐	☐
27. Have you had a serious accident, illness, or surgery?	☐	☐
28. Has anyone in your immediate family died?	☐	☐
29. Have you divorced or separated?	☐	☐

Scoring Key

For each "yes" answer to . . .   Questions 1 to 9: 3 points   Question 28: 6 points
Questions 10 to 22: 4 points   Question 29: 7 points
Questions 23 to 27: 5 points

Interpreting Your Score

1 to 15 points: This range represents a low level of all kinds of stress. If you score in this range, you are probably handling whatever stress you have well.

16 to 40 points: You are experiencing mild to moderate stress. Becoming aware of how much stress you are under may help in relieving some of your built-up anxiety. You may want to watch any future events which might add to your level of stress and delay them if possible.

41 to 117 points: If you scored here, you probably already know you are under stress. You may find it useful to analyze exactly which factors are contributing to your high total. Regardless of what is causing your current stress, it is important to avoid any additional stress until you feel more in control of your life. Second, seek out professional help—your physician or psychologist—for ways to reduce your already high level of stress and for assistance in altering your stress-producing lifestyle.

Source: Journal of Property Management.

Reducing Stress

Stress reduction is vital if the manager is going to achieve the high, long-term productivity needed to excel. There is no one perfect way to reduce stress. However, try a few of the following ideas:

- Take up an exercise or yoga to give stress a physical outlet
- Develop a sense of humor about yourself and your work
- Avoid negative people
- Take up a hobby
- Spend more time with family and friends
- Develop a positive support group to help solve problems
- Give yourself credit for a good job even if no one else does
- Do not rely on alcohol or drugs to relieve stress

By using some or all of these techniques, you can reduce stress on and off the job.

TIME MANAGEMENT

Time is the dimension in which change takes place, just as space is the dimension in which motion takes place. Time is one of our most valuable resources, and we waste much of it. We can buy equipment, rent buildings, and hire personnel, but we cannot buy time. Each person has a finite amount of it and once spent, it is irretrievable. It is perishable and unstorable.

Few people have enough time to do all they want to do. In order, therefore, not to become tense about it, the effective manager learns to use time with respect—to plan how to make the most of it.

A study by a New York recruiting firm* estimated that wasted time costs business $150 billion a year. Employees ''steal'' an average four hours and 22 minutes a week by habitually getting to work late or leaving early, making personal telephone calls, reading, and socializing.

Time management is more than simply not wasting time, which we all do. We forget and are careless and disorganized. Furthermore, it seems unnatural to expect to be 100 percent efficient, like trying to get too much into a suitcase or knapsack. It's easy to spring the lid or burst a seam that way.

A little slack time to relax may be the thing that keeps your psychological or mental seams from bursting. From that point of view, a little wasted time may be self-renewing. Time management, then, does not mean that every minute should be invested in work or study. Some guidelines are as follows:

1. Think about where your time goes. Plan, in writing if possible, how to spend it.
2. Since time is perishable and unstorable, make the most of what you have at the time you have it. Invest your time thoughtfully.

The Wall Street Journal, 27 November, 1984, p. 1.

Time-Management Tips

Much has been written about how to organize time. The following tips have been accumulated over the years from workshops, observation, and reading and can be used by young or old, on or off the job.

1. Allow time to think.
2. Anticipate needs. For example, have on hand an adequate supply of items needed for a task before you start it.
3. Avoid compulsive talkers and people who waste your time.
4. Be a clock watcher. Know where your time goes.
5. Concentrate on the job at hand; one thing at a time.
6. Decide how to spend your time. Set daily, monthly, and even yearly goals.
7. Evaluate the things that claim your time and decide how much each thing is worth. Some are not worth spending time on at all; they have merely become habits.
8. Get an early start. By rising 15–20 minutes early, you get a jump on the whole day.
9. Invest your time where it counts for *you*.
10. Learn to close out distracting sounds and sights, distracting people, and unnecessary interruptions.
11. Learn to say no. Avoid pointless commitments if you can spend the time more profitably.
12. Look for shortcuts and time savers. With a little thought, almost any activity can be simplified. For example, organize your workstation (office, kitchen, or garage) so that less time is lost looking for misplaced things.
13. Learn to recover quickly from interruptions; they eat up time. Some are unavoidable, so when planning the day, allow 3 to 5 percent leeway in your time schedule to provide for interruptions.

14. Phone calls eat up time. When phoning, make notes about items to be discussed. Be pleasant, but eliminate idle chatter.
15. Police leisure time so that you enjoy it to the fullest. For example, be selective about TV shows you watch, the books and magazines you read.
16. Practice good listening. Careful listening saves time otherwise lost checking and rereading. Get it right the first time.
17. Selfishly protect yourself against continuous long hours and overfatigue.
18. Set priorities. Obviously some things must be done before others. Decide what must be done first.
19. Improve your communication skills—writing and talking— so that you do not waste time rewriting or re-explaining.
20. Establish clear goals with co-workers. Sometimes cooperative goal planning takes time initially, but saves time later because it eliminates errors and the repetition of instructions.

LISTENING

A manager's ability to listen effectively is vital to employee morale. It is said that good listeners get ahead, but poor ones make mistakes. Hardly anything builds confidence among employees more than when they realize a supervisor really listens to them. Employees like leaders who listen; they open up to them. Not listening creates many stumbling blocks.

Listening, like writing, talking, and reading, is a skill that can be improved through study and practice. Here are some pointers.

1. To learn to be a good listener, you must recognize the importance of attentive listening and study ways of improving your listening skill.

2. Analyze what constitutes good listening habits, and practice them. For example, ask a speaker to repeat if you are not sure that you heard correctly. Clear up doubtful points at the time by asking questions. Of course, this assumes a one-to-one or a small group situation.
3. Listening uses different skills from reading or writing because words are heard, not seen. When listening, the ears work. One hears voice pitch, pronunciation, and pauses as well as words.
4. When listening, be receptive. Try to keep prejudices or anger from distorting what you hear. Listen objectively, not emotionally.
5. Look for what is positive in a speaker's words—not for what is wrong with them.
6. Hear the speaker out. Listen with as few interruptions as possible even when material is introduced with which you do not agree. Guard against prematurely turning off a speaker as not being worth hearing.
7. Avoid interruptions. Can your telephone calls be channeled elsewhere, for example, when you are meeting and talking with an employee?
8. When listening, search for new things to learn. Retain key ideas; sort out irrelevant comments.
9. When listening to someone who gets bogged down, quietly supply a word or repeat a statement just made to help the speaker.
10. Encourage a speaker by looking at him/her, not at a point in the distance or out the window. Give a speaker the courtesy of undivided attention.
11. In a long conversation, clarify or summarize content briefly by saying, "May I go over a few of the key points to be sure that I understand you correctly?" "Did I understand you correctly? Are you saying that . . .?" "In summary then, what you are saying is. . . ."

12. Effective listening takes energy and self-discipline. Teach yourself to concentrate on what is being said, not on who is saying it or how it is being said. Avoid being distracted by the speaker's clothes or mannerisms.
13. When convenient, make notes. You may want to refer to them later.
14. Keep your own counsel about what you have heard. Your integrity and discretion will inspire confidence.
15. Recognize flattery, name dropping, and sweeping generalizations, yet hear them out, especially if they come from employees or important associates.

Listening Checklist

The following items may help you improve your listening skill. The checklist is not to be scored; it is designed merely to help you review skills associated with good listening and to observe how many of them you practice.

	Yes	*No*
1. Do I give speakers cues that I'm tuned in to what they are saying?	____	____
2. Do I try to communicate an "I'm listening" attitude to the speaker?	____	____
3. Am I aware of my own biases and prejudices so that I am likely to know which ones affect my listening effectiveness?	____	____
4. Do I overreact to words that are emotionally charged for me?	____	____
5. If I disagree with what is being said, do I turn off the speaker?	____	____
6. Do I understand that I need not necessarily agree with a speaker to be a good listener?	____	____
7. Do I recognize that body language and personal attitudes also communicate, thus affecting what I am hearing?	____	____

	Yes	*No*
8. Do I recognize and think about what is not being said?	___	___
9. Do I understand that as a listener, my job is to listen and not to talk? That is, do I understand that when I am talking, I am not listening?	___	___
10. When I have trouble understanding, do I assume the burden of clarification?	___	___
11. Am I a courteous listener?	___	___
12. Do I try to put the speaker at ease?	___	___
13. Can I hear out an emotional or hostile speaker?	___	___
14. Do I try to clarify and summarize at the end of a long conversation or set of instructions?	___	___
15. Do I repeat or discuss (especially if the speaker is a co-worker) instructions for clarification?	___	___
16. Do I ever write down points so that I won't forget them?	___	___

SPEECH

Listening is one aspect of good communication. Learning to effectively convey your ideas to another person is the other side of the coin. Good communication skills are essential to success, in management and in life. By beginning early, communication skills can be learned.

According to Betsy Gilbert, of the Corporate Image, the key to communication is understanding the communication style of the person to whom you are talking. You increase your chances of communicating effectively if you adapt your style to that of your listener.

Determining a person's style requires careful attention to what is said and what is communicated through body language. For example, detail-oriented people may add many facts and figures to their conversation. These people require a great deal of information before they can make a decision.

On the other hand, action-oriented people are often impatient and likely to communicate with few words. They want only enough information to understand the big picture so that they can act. To communicate with action-oriented people, you should highlight the most important features as concisely as possible.

Creative people often enjoy group discussion, which allows for interaction. They may also use you as a sounding board for new ideas. The way to communicate here is to present concepts and options, not just facts.

The words you chose are also an important element in communication. Use simple, straightforward words and a direct tone of voice to ensure that you are understood. Big words may intimidate or confuse a listener.

A good speaking voice is also important, particularly in a business situation. Your voice must have authority, but not be overpowering. Avoid mumbling or including long pauses in your conversation; they lessen your impact as a speaker.

Effective communication is a valuable tool that can benefit any new or experienced manager. Taking courses or joining organizations such as Toastmasters may be valuable in improving this aspect of your management skills.

WRITING

Effective communication also depends on the manager's ability to write well. Whether a manager is called upon to write client proposals, reports to superiors, or simply a business letter, good writing plays an important part in the manager's set of skills.

Writing techniques are fundamentally the same for all types of written documents. However, for the purposes of this chapter, we will use the business letter as an example.

The first step in good writing is to define the objective of the piece being written. What do you want to do? Do you need to convey information? Must you get someone to act in a certain way? Are you trying to build goodwill? You should be able to state your writing goal before you ever put pen to paper.

In writing, as in speaking, keeping it simple is always best. Avoid using a complex word when a basic one will work just as well. Write "use" instead of "utilize," "try" instead of "endeavor," "understand" instead of "ascertain."

Simple writing also helps the writer avoid wordiness and unnecessarily complex sentences. A study of Yale undergraduates recently pointed out the effectiveness of shorter sentences in increasing comprehension. Comprehension rose from 18 percent to 93 percent when sentences with 18 words or less and paragraphs of five to seven sentences were used.

Writing is an extension of yourself. A manager who writes well can do a good job more easily and will be more readily recognized by others as effective.

CHAPTER 8

JOB-HUNTING STRATEGIES

By the time you finish school, you should have selected a career and the type of organization in which you want to work. Many books and magazines provide occupational information. *The Occupational Outlook Handbook,* found in most libraries and school guidance offices, has helpful job descriptions and suggestions. Don't overlook government literature which describes a wide range of employment opportunities. Learn about government jobs in your state and neighboring ones. That may be where you find your career. There's one out there for everyone who wants to work and who prepares for it.

Employment agencies and temporary services provide fill-in jobs which give you experience while you are looking for that special opening. Temporary services can place you in the type of firms in which you ultimately want to work. This sort of experience is especially helpful if you are young and inexperienced. Some entry-level jobs require no specific skills and give you a chance to gain self-confidence.

TEMPORARY SERVICES

Today, most large companies use temporary employees, and the status of temporary employees has risen. Educational levels of people working for temporary companies have increased. In addition, more professional and technical workers, such as accountants and computer analysts, are available on a temporary basis. This development has also helped improve the standard of temporary employment.

There are many advantages to working for a temporary employment company. A worker can explore the work environments of different companies and can gain experience in many kinds of structures. Temporary workers are often offered permanent jobs or references for other job applications. It's important to realize that some temporary companies require an employee to work for them for a minimum period of time—perhaps two or three months. However, if a company offers a full-time job that the temp employee wants to accept, an arrangement can be made with the temporary company.

Another advantage for workers who have recently relocated is that temporary firms send their workers to various parts of the city, if the workers so desire. You can make arrangements to work only in a certain area, but if you are new in town, you may want to try out various locations. In this way, you will get to know the transportation system, the characteristics of various neighborhoods, and the travel time required from your home.

It's wise to get basic information before you begin an assignment. Ask about travel routes, public transportation, the safety of various areas, and where to eat lunch. The agent at the temporary employment firm can advise you. If that person seems short on information, ask another. Be sure you know where you are going and the basic facts about the area before you start out. A temporary job can be an adventure in miniature, but it can be too much of an adventure if you find yourself in a strange neighborhood at 5:00

P.M. on a winter evening, with no buses running and no pay phones within sight. If you decide to explore the job market via the temporary employment route, make a list of the information you will need, and be sure your questions are answered before you leave on the assignment.

For the prospective manager, getting early work experience with a temporary company has the special advantage of allowing you to observe many different management techniques in action. Obviously, you will not be able to study them in depth, but you will see the effects of management that is too strict, too loose, too uninformed, or too hasty. You can observe carefully, and learn a great deal in a short time, if you become sophisticated enough to quietly make comparisons and remember what you observe. This is not to say that you can pry into a company's affairs—even if you work for a company for a single day, you still have an ethical responsibility to observe the rights of confidentiality. However, you have a right to think about what you experience, and you can make the most of it for your own education.

OTHER JOB LEADS

Employment agencies are another way to find your first job. Some employment and search firm agencies handle only special job categories. These may include travel agents, computer operators and programmers, property managers, or at higher levels, even candidates for boards of directors. Some search firms specialize in helping corporations find qualified members of industrial, financial, and business boards.

Other sources of job information are newspapers, campus bulletin boards, campus placement offices, and friends and relatives. A large percentage of job seekers get their best leads through other people. An annual average of about 270,000 openings for managers and administrators is predicted for the next few years. This includes bank officials, financial managers, wholesale and retail buyers, shippers of farm products, building managers, and corporate department managers. On the whole, the market for management trainees continues to be promising.

HOW TO BEGIN

Begin with a job-hunting plan that includes such items as type of community in which you want to work (size of the town, climate), the type of organization or industry you prefer and are most prepared to enter, and the corporate department (marketing, finance, production) in which you want to begin. Write out the information so that you can see and think about it. Consider why you want to work in the type of firm you selected and why you want to move to another area, if you do. If your plan means moving to another part of the country, subscribe to a newspaper from that area, especially the Sunday edition, and watch classified ads. The *Wall Street Journal* and the *New York Times* carry a wide range of classified ads which include jobs for areas all over the country.

WHERE TO LOOK

When you begin to look for a job, be optimistic and confident. Enjoy the experience, confident that someplace there is a right job for you. If you approach job hunting with fear and worry, you will communicate some of your anxiety and uncertainty. If you do not have confidence in yourself, how can you expect others to develop confidence in your ability? You are not the first person to go job hunting. Everyone who works has had the experience, including the person who interviews you.

If your school has an employment interview center, register with it. If it has a vocational guidance center, use it. The more people who talk to you about your job hunt, the more points of view you get.

The vocational guidance clinic at your school may suggest that you take a battery of tests (personality, aptitude, interest, and so forth). Do not shy away from them. Consider them to be another learning experience. Large corporations sometimes use similar tests when trying to match individuals with available opportunities. It is possible that some published and standardized tests you take in the vocational guidance clinic are also used by corporations that interest you, so welcome any chance to take these tests. In fact, you might want to read about published and standardized tests in the library.

Taking tests may be compared to falling off a horse. The more experience you have, the less likely you are to be upset by it. Standardized tests help you learn about yourself—your abilities, strengths, and weaknesses.

Next, read newspaper ads and register with employment agencies: private, public, civil service, school placement centers, and in-company employment departments. Even the yellow pages of a phone book or the city directory may help you find the right employer.

Check the trade journals, and when you read about a company that sounds good to you, write to them, even if they are not advertising the type of job you want. You might make a list of companies that interest you, using *Dun and Bradstreet* and similar business directories in the library. Mail a resume letter which gives just enough information to identify you—not an actual resume. Address the letter to the personnel manager, and ask for an interview.

When replying to a newspaper ad, since a post-office number is usually the only address given, emphasize your desire to have an interview, to talk with them personally. Make arranging an interview with the hiring official easy by listing several dates and specific times when you are available.

When you register with an employment agency, whether private or public, you will be given an application form to complete. Read it through so that you understand the fee expected (if any) and other terms included. Then, in ink or with a typewriter, if one is available, complete the form as accurately and neatly as possible. You may want to attach a copy of your full resume.

Many employment agencies belong to the National Association of Personnel Consultants. If you desire a list of members (close to two thousand all over the country), write to the National Association of Personnel Consultants, 1432 Duke Street, Alexandria, Virginia 22314.

STEPS TO TAKE AS AN APPLICANT

After you find an advertisement or get a job lead, follow these steps:

1. Call the business and make an appointment for a job interview. If the ad gives only a box number, write for an appointment. Enclose a copy of your resume.
2. Proceed to the appointment appropriately dressed and ready to answer questions. Be prepared to explain why you are applying for that particular job.
3. If you are interviewed by several people, talk to counselors, or are taken to lunch or for a coffee break, continue to answer questions frankly but as briefly as possible. Be friendly, but keep a professional distance.
4. If you are asked to take standardized tests, do so as graciously as possible. Of course, ask necessary clarification questions.

5. If you are given an application form, use a pen (your own) and block print the items, especially if your handwriting is hard to read.

CLASSIFIED ADS

Assume that you find the following two ads in the newspaper:

Ad No. 1

RESTAURANT MANAGERS, EXPERIENCED OR
ENTRY-LEVEL
Come to our open house, Sunday, June 17
9 am to 4 pm
and learn what it means to become one of our managers. We are expanding and invite you to explore the opportunity to operate one of our restaurants anywhere in the U.S.

If you are energetic, mature, hard working and have management/supervisory knowledge or experience, come meet us. We can offer you:
- starting salary commensurate with experience and ability
- opportunity for professional advancement
- state-of-the-art training
- a five-day work week
- excellent benefits
- an opportunity to realize short- and long-term career goals

If you cannot attend our open house at Bradford Inn, 3685 Bradford Way, Lincolnville, Ill 60646, mail your resume. We are an equal opportunity employer.

Ad No. 2

WANTED: MANAGEMENT TRAINEES IN FINANCIAL SERVICES

We are among the nation's leading property and casualty insurers and are looking for exceptional men and women to train for positions of significant management and technical responsibility.

If you like a challenge and have the drive to succeed, send us a resume that looks something like this:

Objective: To secure a position in a high-potential trainee program.

Education: A bachelor's degree with a major in insurance, finance, accounting, economics, or management.

Experience: 0-2 years, preferably in a business environment.

Personal: An achiever, energetic and articulate, able to communicate with all levels of management.

Geographic Preference: Will locate anywhere

(Dept JSR 9, XYZ Co., 902 E. Murdok Ave, Suite 2272, Grovedale, CO 80011)

RESUMES

Assume that you are interested in interviewing for one of these jobs and will mail a resume as requested. Can you write a good resume? Assume that the ad you answer brings responses from over a hundred applicants. Will your resume receive favorable attention? If it will stand out from the others, what will make it special? Will it land in the wastebasket or bring you an invitation for a special interview?

Learn to write a good resume. Get help if you need it from former teachers, knowledgeable friends, former bosses, and from samples in books. The result will be worth the extra effort. Study illustrations. Can you improve upon them to suit your purpose? Sometimes a very distinctive stationery may be helpful; or a bright blue or green typewriter ribbon. You may want to fold the stationery so that the resume opens out like a folder. The style you use should be appropriate to the kind of job you want.

Use the following suggestions in preparing your resume.

1. A resume should always be typed and, of course, absolutely free of errors, strikeovers, and noticeable corrections. Do not mail carbon copies. Use originals; printed copies or photocopies are acceptable. An otherwise good resume can be ruined by a sloppy appearance.

2. Consider accompanying a resume of purely factual statistics (easy to read) with a short cover letter that introduces you (name, type of job you want) and says that the attached resume or personal data sheet describes your education, job experience, special attributes, and expertise.

3. Personal data may, if you choose, include age, height, weight, marital status and/or dependents. If recently divorced, merely say ''single.'' You may also want to touch on disabilities, if you have any. Mention whether you will travel or relocate as opportunities arise.

4. When describing education, start with the highest credential earned. Describe the types of schools attended (night school, correspondence, university extension, company sponsored, trade apprenticeship, military). If you have gone beyond high school but do not have a degree, indicate the credit hours earned to date, rather than the number of years or terms. Include minor fields of educational interest as well as your major.

5. Try to put your best foot forward when describing your experience, but do not exaggerate. Start with the job most recently held, including the name of the company, city and state in which it is located, and job title. Give the month as well as the year in the date. It may help if you give a short, snappy list of job responsibilities and duties. Use action verbs—such as handled, organized, developed—that tell what you did.

6. Be as truthful as possible about why you left a job. It pays in the long run; false job facts have a way of catching up with you. If you were fired, say so, and give the reason: "Dismissed—could not agree with the supervisor." Don't go into further detail because you want to be extremely careful about criticizing anyone. Personnel managers find it refreshing to see the truth set forth but don't want grubby details.

7. Use a highlighter pen to spotlight special items in your resume or data sheet. Another way to emphasize is to make arrows or insert key words ("Please note") in the margin with a distinctively colored felt-tip pen.

8. Include a "Remarks" section for such items as extracurricular activities (and offices held), languages spoken, membership(s) in professional organizations (offices held), travel experience, when available for an interview, and any other information you think might help you and the interviewer. You should feel free to note your best qualities, describing yourself as "easy to work with," "enjoy responsibility and new projects," and so forth.

9. Job hunters often ask about personal references. Open letters of recommendation are not very useful, and even if you have some from former teachers or employers, they should not be attached to the resume. Instead, indicate that references are available upon request. Of course, you will,

whenever possible, get a reference's permission. You may save yourself embarrassment by doing so.

10. Another often asked question concerns including a photograph of yourself. Business resumes should not include a photo.

INTERVIEWS

If you get that sought-after interview, go to it prepared. Be prepared to give them the facts they want. Give them a good, relaxed, friendly view of yourself. Remember, you are enjoying your job-hunting experience, confident that the perfect job for you exists somewhere.

To some extent, an interview is a moment of truth. Getting the job will probably depend on it. Unfortunately, your success may hinge on whether the interviewer likes you, on what kind of a first impression you make. So, instead of dreading the interview and thinking of it as an ordeal, treat it as the very important opportunity it is. Plan for it; think about items you want to clarify or emphasize; take copies of your resume and samples of your work; rest so that you look well; be alert; be aware of how much good attitudes and a good appearance may help you during an interview. This interview may be one of the most important events of your life.

Usually an interviewer, through job descriptions and specifications, has a pretty good idea of what the company is seeking. Here are a few things to think about as you prepare for an interview:

1. The first glimpse the interviewer has of you is important. If it is unfavorable, it may be hard to counteract.
2. Before you leave for an interview, take a good look at yourself in a full-length mirror. Would you hire what you see?

RESUME (suggested arrangement)	
PERSONAL	Lee F. Johnson 4518 Crane Avenue Pleasantville, Wisconsin 53538 (555) 123-1234
OBJECTIVE	Responsible work in administration with emphasis on marketing and analytical aspects. Aim to combine initial staff work with opportunity for long-term growth in an organization. Willing to relocate.
EDUCATION	Henderson Community College. Henderson, Wisconsin. Associate degree (1983) in business management with a concentration in marketing. Scholastic average 3.1 (A = 4). Henderson Senior High School, 1981; major in business and accounting. Scholastic average 3.4.
EXPERIENCE	General Food Services (statewide chain), Henderson. Part-time and summer, 1981 to present. Assistant and relief store manager, 1982 to present. Responsibilities: troubleshooting, sales promotions, inventory and shipments, interviewing new employees, scheduling employees, handling deposits, checking store before lock-up time.
ACTIVITIES	Vice-president of marketing club; advertising manager, *Henderson Hack* (school newspaper).
MEMBERSHIPS	American Marketing Association.
REFERENCES	Information on file, Henderson Community College placement office. Other available on request.

The Confidential Resume of	13446 Briarway
Lee F. Johnson	Utica, New York 10097
	(555) 123-1234

OBJECTIVE — Supervisory management career, manufacturing organization, medium size.

EDUCATION — New York State University, Albany, New York 1971 to 1974. Earned B.S. degree in accounting and finance.

EXPERIENCE — Miller and Snyder, Inc., office manager reporting to J.D. Snyder. This firm did contracting and area development work. After two years and good results as office manager, I became corporate secretary in the Utica home office, bought company stock, and got a good bonus. When Miller and Snyder sold the controlling interest to a large Buffalo, New York–based firm, the reorganization did not include me.

MILITARY — Coast Guard Reserve, Ensign.

REMARKS — Am considered to be stable, dependable, and get along well with those who report to me. I am buying a home in Utica.

SALARY — $45,000 to $50,000 desired.

REFERENCES — Good business and personal references available upon request, especially from Mr. J. D. Snyder, Miller and Snyder, Inc.

3. When interviewing, be conservative. Let the right "you" shine through. If you appear too different, you will distract the interviewer, so avoid extremes of dress and scent. It is worth the effort. After all, you want the job, or you would not be there. After you get the job and your co-workers get to know you, you can let up a little and be less conservative. But remember, good appearance reflects your personality and tells the interviewer you would be a dependable, quality employee.

4. When talking, look the interviewer in the eyes and, if seated, sit up.

5. Check your attitude as you prepare for an interview. Are you ready to meet the interviewer more than half way, or are you going to use the opportunity to display the chip you may be carrying on your shoulder?

6. Even when you find you do not want the job for which you are interviewing, try to leave a good impression; make a friend. You cannot tell when you may meet or need that friend. Make a real effort to be pleasant and friendly.

7. Each interview is an experience and an opportunity. Learn from it so that your next interview is that much better as a result.

8. Speak up. Take the initiative in talking if the interview seems to lag, but do not chatter too much. Try to recognize signals that the interview is ending, for example, when the interviewer stands up. Try not to overstay your welcome.

9. Think through beforehand a few questions you may want to ask. For example: "What would my most important responsibilities be?" "Does the company have an educational program?" or "I'm eager to have a real business career. Do you think this position can be a stepping stone for me if I do well?"

10. Learn as much as you can about the company beforehand. It will help you ask meaningful questions. Interviewers are trained to invite candidates to ask questions. Questions a candidate asks can be a revealing source of information, especially about poise, verbal ability, attitudes, and qualifications.

11. If you feel unsure about your ability to ask questions during an interview or to take the initiative should the interview lag, practice on your family or friends. You might also practice before a mirror. Look directly at the other person, not at a spot overhead. Try out your smile, a few hand gestures, and different tones of voice. Be sure to speak up and enunciate so that you can be heard and understood.

12. Remember that you are being watched and evaluated during an interview. Therefore, if an unexpected question is asked, answer briefly and in a natural and friendly manner. Try not to ramble or get off the subject.

13. When the interview is over, leave in a cheerful, friendly way. Ask when you may expect to hear the result. Thank the interviewer as you leave, even if you do not think you will get the job. When you get home, it is a good idea to write the interviewer a formal letter of thanks.

14. What kind of handshake do you have? Is it limp and lifeless? Practice a firm, cordial grip. Use it, especially when you leave an interview, even if you think it did not go well. This applies for females as well as males. The day when women did not offer to shake hands with men is long gone.

15. Don't let yourself become upset during an interview. The interviewer may be testing your self-control. If a question or comment really annoys you, turn it aside with a smile, a humorous remark, or a direct friendly answer. You have everything to lose if you lose your cool; the interviewer has nothing to lose.

16. An interview is a one-to-one relationship. The interviewer is simply another employee of the company doing a job. If for some reason you find yourself reacting negatively to an interviewer, try not to form your opinion of the company accordingly. There are likely to be many types of people in an organization and, obviously, you will not like them all.

YOUR FUTURE

Every day hundreds of people are out interviewing or starting new careers. There are thousands of opportunities, and one of them is for you. Occasionally the only job available is part-time or seasonal. If you like the company, take the job, even if it is not quite what you want. Do not turn down a job because it is not in the department you prefer. You never know what a job may lead to, especially if it is with the type of company that interests you.

Some employment agencies specialize in supplying businesses with part-time, fill-in employees. If you have free time, sign up and interview with such an agency. It is an excellent way to get experience and to observe a variety of job settings.

If you get a promising job offer while still in school, think carefully before you decide to drop out of school to take it. Is this the type of job you want for the rest of your life? There are many years and opportunities ahead of you. Think about your personal preferences, goals, and dreams. Will the job being offered help you fulfill your dreams?

Each day brings new opportunities. Envision the years ahead. What will you be doing in twenty years, and what do you want to do between now and then? The future is yours. You can do much to mold and control it if you think ahead, planning and preparing so that you can take advantage of opportunities that come your way. Don't let yourself become bogged down with idle companions, time-killing pastimes, lazy habits, or self-pity. Stay on top, realizing that there will be some disappointments and setbacks. Use even these as learning situations and stepping stones, so that when you reach your later years, you can look back with few regrets and feel good about your career and your life.

CHAPTER 9

NEW DIMENSIONS
FOR TOMORROW'S MANAGERS

Everyone, at some time or other, wonders about the future. As one of tomorrow's managers, what awaits you?

HUMANISM

In the past twenty years we have seen continuous emphasis in the United States on human rights, equal opportunities, and improved standards of living so that more people may enjoy better lives. Workers of all kinds are looking for more challenge and opportunity and materially richer and more comfortable lives, including more recreation and travel. At the same time, business and government strive to maintain prosperity and increase production while meeting problems of growing populations, inflation, food distribution, diminishing resources, environmental concerns, and accelerating competition for world markets. Decreasing our national debt, maintaining a balance of trade, and assuring the survival of U.S. industries are a few of the problems that face tomorrow's managers.

INTERNATIONALISM

With parts, supplies, and produce coming from all over the world, any narrow provincialism in American business management is a thing of the past. Even in supermarkets, for example, grapes come from Chile, oranges from Israel, oysters from Korea, and sardines from Norway. Manufacturers have assembly plants in Mexico, Spain, and the Far East. Firms are expanding into Brazil, China, and many other countries as they seek new markets.

Business schools play up globalism by adding new courses in internationalism to their curricula. Titles of new courses added for MBAs include "The Environment of International Business," "Focusing on World Problems," and "Doing Business Abroad." Finance courses consider problems in foreign trade. Fluctuations between the U.S. dollar and foreign currencies can cost corporations millions of dollars. For some companies, significant parts of their total revenue now come from sales outside the United States. American management teams of the future will include foreign market surveillance experts.

Managers are spending more time on wheels and in the air. It is not unusual even for a senior officer to fly 250,000 miles and more a year, personally checking new market developments abroad and in the United States.

Maintaining contact with new ventures in an expanding world market requires a strong commitment from management which, in the final analysis, is responsible to customers and stockholders. Of course, senior officers must be able to depend on other managers' eyes and ears because they cannot spend much time traveling to make firsthand contacts. However, as corporations spread throughout the world, it becomes harder to coordinate information from the different branches. Fortunately, computers help to retain and digest information coming from these many sources, but business experts expect new types of organization with more independent profit centers and local accountability in order to create more of a community feeling. Corporations will organize into smaller operating units. Telecommunication among the units, and between the units and the parent company, will facilitate this type of organization. Tomorrow's managers will break with many management practices that have been accepted for decades and develop new ones to meet the needs of the time. The tempo of world events will not permit managers to control affairs primarily from reports and financial statements passed to them by line personnel and lower levels of management. Tomorrow's manager must keep in closer touch with events and people because things are moving too fast, and there is too much competition out there.

AGE

The aging of the baby boom generation is creating another form of competition—a bottleneck of employees in their thirties and forties who are ready to move into middle and upper management. Workers between the ages of 35 and 54 will account for 49 percent of the labor force by the year 2000. This increases competition for management jobs and is likely to keep somewhat older managers in supervisory positions longer. Chances for younger people to move into management will be limited.

In addition, as some companies extend retirement age above 65 years, older managers may remain in jobs longer. This tendency will also limit promotion opportunities for those eager to move up the corporate ladder. However, this pattern is somewhat counteracted by a trend among managers in their late fifties and early sixties to retire early.

The decline in the number of people in the 20-to-25 age group should offer more options for those entering business. In addition, the number in this group will continue to decline for a decade.

Age Distribution of the Labor Force

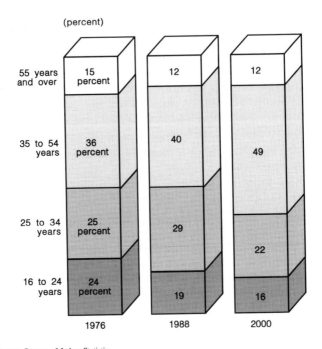

(percent)

	1976	1988	2000
55 years and over	15 percent	12	12
35 to 54 years	36 percent	40	49
25 to 34 years	25 percent	29	22
16 to 24 years	24 percent	19	16

Source: Bureau of Labor Statistics

Thus entry into college, graduates schools, and management training courses will probably be easier than it was a decade ago.

APPREHENSIONS

Many American employees, managers as well as workers, continue to find it unsettling to cope with current changes. They worry about what sophisticated technology and new scientific discoveries are doing to the world and to the human race. They are restless about their jobs. An AMACOM survey concluded that "fear of success seems to be a universal problem" and that "human beings have a limited tolerance for receiving goodness, pleasure, and joy." You may not agree with this conclusion entirely; yet you have probably observed some of these characteristics in yourself or your friends. When things are going really well, people get apprehensive and fear that it may be a lull before the storm. If you look for trouble, it usually is not hard to find. This generalization applies to personal situations as well as to work environments.

Another reason for apprehension is that technology has given increased power to machines, especially computers. How does mechanizing and automating so much work affect creativity, which is a fundamental human urge? This dilemma challenges management to find outlets for employee creativity and to keep operators interested in their work—to keep them motivated. One new idea for doing so is to involve workers continually in decision making.

COMPUTERS

Microcomputers are among the most startling inventions of the last decades of the twentieth century. They have grown from a specialized piece of machinery to standard office equipment in fewer than ten years. Most graduate management programs now require students to own a personal computer as an admission requirement.

Today's and tomorrow's manager must be completely comfortable operating a personal computer. Whether a manager is engaged in financial analysis, record keeping, budgeting, communications, or specialized activities related to a specific industry, that work will probably be done on a computer. The increasingly widespread use of computers also continues to create opportunities for computer programmers and analysts, which will be among the fastest growing professions in the 1990s.

DIVERSIFICATION AND EXPANSION

Progress is a law of economic life. When a firm ceases to progress, it starts to fall back. Competition is so keen that if a company stops progressing for even a short time, it may never catch up again. New products, new services, and new production methods evolve almost daily. New products and businesses appear, and others, having become obsolete, quietly disappear. A large percentage of what is sold in supermarkets today was practically unheard of a couple of decades ago.

No manager is valuable to a company's success unless he or she can help that company move ahead and progress. Sometimes this progress involves diversification of product and expansion, even into foreign markets. At other times, it means retracting, getting rid of declining products and ineffective personnel—what in nautical terms is called "trimming the sails." Tomorrow's managers must be even more expert at making changes than today's because the rate of change in business organization, product distribution, and technology is accelerating. The manager who becomes bogged down in routine is courting disaster. There are raiders out there who sense when an organization is faltering and close in for a takeover "kill." A company must progress at all levels in order to survive successfully in today's competitive market.

At the line level, supervisors must be alert to production changes; at the middle-management level, managers must be quick to facilitate changes developed at the top; and at the senior-management level, executives must develop new ideas and courses of action for building new lines, expanding active ones, and getting a fair share of the market.

THE ACTUALIZING ORGANIZATION

To provide a creative environment for tomorrow's employees, managers need to consider such guidelines as the following:

1. Provide review and goal-setting sessions at all levels of the organization.
2. Get information input from the grass-root levels—clerical and plant production.
3. Use matrix-mix employee teams for review and problem-solving sessions.
4. Strive for an interaction of good minds in the organization.
5. Encourage individuality and creativity among employees. Affirm the worth of the individual.
6. Encourage self-actualization among employees.
7. Think of product and profit growth as the result of people and process growth.
8. See profit as a means of maintaining a healthy, progressive organization and not as an end in itself.
9. Assume social responsibility, locally and abroad, whenever practical opportunities present themselves. Take a global view.
10. Clarify the philosophical base from which the company's managers function.
11. Discourage ''status gaps'' in the organization.
12. Assign responsibility on the basis of competence rather than status.
13. Recognize that management's integrity is essential to a company's long-range success.

14. Experiment with in-house mentor and sponsorship programs.
15. Regard information as a commodity like iron or steel. It can be used to reinforce the structure of the organization.
16. Recognize that good communication, like finance and production, is an underpinning of a strong company.

It should be obvious that tomorrow's actualizing organizations will have managers who know how to get results in an increasingly competitive international business environment. Such managers encourage everyone in the firm to contribute, unafraid that management's authority will be threatened.

THE ACTUALIZING EXECUTIVE

The actualizing executive has these qualities:

1. Sets flexible goals and objectives so that when new circumstances dictate a change it can be made.
2. Is a whole person with compassion for humanity.
3. Is challenged to high levels of performance.
4. Can visualize the way things should be and prepares for the future, even when ahead of the times.
5. Welcomes intellectual conflict as a sign of thinking interest.
6. Respects opinions of colleagues and subordinates, realizing that progress is usually the fruit of thought—and labor.
7. Tries to eliminate status gaps so that employees can communicate constructively regardless of job titles. Encourages friendly informality.
8. Sets up situations that develop and release human initiative in the organization.

9. Recognizes the importance of the profit motive but does not consider it to be an end to which all human values must be sacrificed.
10. Practices positive reinforcement by recognizing good performance more often than disciplining employees for poor performance.
11. Recognizes risk as an important ingredient in growth and innovation.
12. Communicates up, down, and across organizational lines.
13. Recognizes that the quality of an organization can be no better than the minds of its managers.
14. Recognizes physical fitness as an important part of mental health.

ENVIRONMENTALISM

Today, organizations are more concerned abut their impact on the physical environment than in the past. Concern about the environment will be even greater in the future because of an increasing awareness that the earth's ecology is fragile.

Some of the ecological controls now in effect are hard to implement, such as the recall of thousands of cars to replace emission controls. Tomorrow's managers must be ready to combat such problems because business organizations care about their social image as well as their social responsibilities. Many companies spend a great deal of money on institutional advertising and image enhancement. A company with a good reputation for quality products, good service, and fair prices is, understandably, eager to protect it.

PREPARING FOR TOMORROW

The environment in which tomorrow's managers function will probably include some of the following challenges:

1. New management practices
2. More demanding and articulate employees
3. An unsettled political and world environment with international conflicts
4. Stress
5. Early obsolescence
6. Fluctuations in the economy
7. The technological revolution
8. Change
9. Radically different life-styles
10. Competition

As we approach the next century, new management theories and concepts emerge too numerous to discuss in a book of this size and type. They combine sociology, psychology, philosophy, and science.

Everything that happens anywhere in the world has an impact on us. It will be no small challenge for managers to stay on top of the happenings and to anticipate their impact. Management is a very demanding profession, but the potential rewards are rich and to participate from the front lines of leadership can be exciting and fulfilling.

Arnold Toynbee, world-renowned philosopher, historian, and writer reminds us that of twenty-one past great civilizations, nineteen crumbled from within; only two were conquered from without. Many believe that our civilization is crumbling. All forces, including business, government, and educators, must unite to keep our society strong and healthy despite the complex problems we face today. Managers at every level and in every type of organization should think about their impact on society and the economy. They must try, for example, to understand the impact their products have on civilization.

Tomorrow's business manager has an opportunity to be an influence for world good. Profit must not be the main incentive. The world has shrunk too much for that—and it's extremely crowded! There are other important needs besides profit, other things that need attention from the people who are trained to organize, administer, and manage. The challenge for tomorrow's manager includes the responsibility to produce goods and services that benefit civilization without harming the environment that supports it.

APPENDIX A

BIBLIOGRAPHY

Association of Management Consulting Firms. *ACME Survey of Key Management Information.* New York, 1988.

Adler, Nancy J. and Dafna N. Izraeli, eds. *Women in Management.* Armonk, NY: M.E. Sharpe, Inc., 1988.

AMACOM. *Decision-Making for the First-Time Manager,* by William Weis. New York, 1989.

————. *Executive Productivity,* by Herman S. Jacobs with Katherine Jillson. New York, 1974.

————. *The First Time Manager,* by Loren B. Belker. New York, 1986.

————. *How American Chief Executives Succeed,* by Charles Margerison and Andrew Kakabadse. New York, 1984.

————. *The Inner Game of Management: How to Make a Managerial Role,* by Eric Flamholtz. New York, 1987.

————. *Loud and Clear: A Guide to Effective Communication,* by Sy Lazarus. 1981.

————. *Managerial Values in Perspective,* by Warren H. Schmidt and Barry Z. Posner. New York, 1983.

————. *Manager to Manager II: What Managers Think of Their Managerial Careers,* by Robert F. Pearse. New York, 1977.

————. *Middle Management Morale in the '80s,* by George E. Breen. New York, 1983.

American Association of Collegiate Schools of Business and the European Foundation of Management Development Staff, eds. *Management for the 21st Century.* Norwell, MA: Kluwer Academic Publishers, 1982.

129

Baehler, James R. *The New Manager's Guide to Success*. Westport, CT: Praeger Publishers, 1980.

Bolles, Richard Nelson. *What Color Is Your Parachute?* Berkeley, CA: Ten Speed Press, 1989.

Centron, Marvin J. with Marcia Appel. *Jobs of the Future*. McGraw Hill Book Company, 1984.

Domkowski, Dorothy and Lila B. Stair. *Careers in Business*. Lincolnwood, IL: VGM Career Horizons, 1986.

Greenwood, James, Jr. and James Greenwood, III. *Managing Executive Stress*. Tenafly, NJ: Burrill Ellsworth, 1984.

Gutek, Barbara and Laurie Larwood, eds. *Women's Career Development*. Newbury Park, PA: Sage Publishing, 1987.

Hall, Douglas T., et. al. *Career Development in Organizations*. San Francisco: Jossey-Bass, 1986.

Hill, William. *Management in Action: Guidelines for New Managers*. Battelle, 1985.

Holton, Ed. *The MBA's Guide to Career Planning*. Princeton, NJ: Peterson's Guides, 1989.

Lewis, Adele and William Lewis. *Getting a Job in Today's Competitive Market*. Hauppause, NY: Barron's Educational Series, 1982.

Lott, Catherine S. and Oscar C. Lott. *How to Land a Better Job*. Lincolnwood, IL: VGM Career Horizons, 1989.

McBurney, William J., Jr. *Where the Jobs Are*. Radnor, PA: Chilton Book Company, 1982.

Reardon, Patrick and Kirby W. Stanat. *Job Hunting Secrets and Tactics*. Piscataway, NJ: New Century/Westwind, 1977.

Shore, Howard F., ed. *Start Supervising*. 3d ed. Washington, DC: BNA, 1984.

Sonnerfeld, Jeffrey. *Managing Career Systems: Channeling the Flow of an Executive Career*. Irwin, 1984.

State Mutual Bank. *Your Guide to Job Promotion*, by John H. Mepham. New York: 1987.

Vroom, Cynthia, et. al., eds. *A Directory of Career Resources for Minorities*. Alvey Publishing, 1984.

Wright, John W. *The American Almanac of Jobs and Salaries*. New York: Avon Books, 1987.

MANAGEMENT ASSOCIATIONS

The list below presents a selection of management associations in various career fields. There are many more, and you will want to consult a directory of associations, as well as other reference materials at the time you wish to research various organizations for your career plans. Your local librarian can help you to select from the many good reference materials available.

Administrative Management Society
   4622 Street Road
   Trevose, Pennsylvania 19047

American Accounting Association
   5717 Bessie Drive
   Sarasota, Florida 34233

American Advertising Federation
   1400 K Street, NW
   Washington, D.C. 20005

American Association of Hispanic CPAs
   1414 Metropolitan Avenue
   Bronx, New York 10462

American Bankers Association
   1120 Connecticut Avenue, NW
   Washington, D.C. 20036

American Council of Life Insurance
   1001 Pennsylvania Avenue, NW
   Washington, D.C. 20004

American Institute of Certified Public Accountants
   1211 Avenue of the Americas
   New York, New York 10036

American Management Association
   135 W. Fiftieth Street
   New York, New York 10020

American Marketing Association
   250 S. Wacker Drive
   Chicago, Illinois 60606

American Production and Inventory Control Society
   500 W. Annandale Road
   Falls Church, Virginia 22046

American Society of Information Science
   1424 Sixteenth Street, NW
   Washington, D.C. 20036

American Society for Personnel Administration
   606 N. Washington Street
   Alexandria, Virginia 22314

American Society for Quality Control
   310 W. Wisconsin Avenue
   Milwaukee, Wisconsin 53203

American Society for Training and Development
   1630 Duke Street
   Alexandria, Virginia 22313

American Society of Association Executives
   1575 I Street, NW
   Washington, D.C. 20005

American Society of Pension Actuaries
   2029 K Street, NW
   Washington, D.C. 20006

American Society of Women Accountants
35 E. Wacker Drive
Chicago, Illinois 60601

American Stock Exchange
Information Services Division
86 Trinity Place
New York, New York 10006

Asian American Certified Public Accountants
P.O. Box 26850
San Francisco, California 94126

Association for Systems Management
24587 Bagley Road
Cleveland, Ohio 44138

Association of Managing Consultants
19 W. Forty-fourth Street
New York, New York 10036

Association of Part-Time Professionals
7655 Old Springhouse Road
McLean, Virginia 22102

Bank Administration Institute
60 Gould Center
Rolling Meadows, Illinois 60008

Coalition of Minority Women in Business
1535 P Street, NW
Washington, D.C. 20005

Construction Management Association of America
12355 Sunrise Valley Drive
Reston, Virginia 22091

Credit Union National Association, Inc.
P.O. Box 431
Madison, Wisconsin 53701

Executive Women International
965 E. 4800 Street
Salt Lake City, Utah 84117

Industrial Relations Research Association
  7226 Social Science Building
  University of Wisconsin
  Madison, Wisconsin 53706

Institute of Certified Management Accountants
  10 Paragon Drive
  Montvale, New Jersey 07645

Institute of Certified Managers
  James Madison University
  Harrisonburg, Virginia 22807

Institute of Internal Auditors, Inc.
  249 Maitland Avenue
  Altamonte Springs, Florida 32701

Institute of Real Estate Management
  430 N. Michigan Avenue
  Chicago, Illinois 60611

International Food Service Executives Association
  3017 W. Charleston Boulevard
  Las Vegas, Nevada 89102

International Franchise Association
  1350 New York Avenue, NW
  Washington, D.C. 20005

Marketing Communications International
  4901 Woodall Street
  Dallas, Texas 75247

Manufacturers' Agents National Association
  P.O. Box 3467
  Laguna Hills, California 92654

Medical Group Management Association
  1355 S. Colorado Boulevard
  Denver, Colorado 80222

National Association of Accountants
  10 Paragon Drive
  Montvale, New Jersey 07645

National Association of Bank Women, Inc.
500 N. Michigan Avenue
Chicago, Illinois 60611

National Association of Black Accountants
300 I Street, NE
Washington, D.C. 20002

National Association of Credit Management
520 Eighth Avenue
New York, New York 10018

National Association of Independent Insurers
2600 River Road
Des Plaines, Illinois 60018

National Association of Insurance Brokers
1401 New York Avenue, NW
Washington, DC 20005

National Association of Insurance Women International
P.O. Box 4410
Tulsa, Oklahoma 74159

National Association of Purchasing Management
P.O. Box 22160
Tempe, Arizona 85282

National Association of State Purchasing Officials
P.O. Box 11910
Lexington, Kentucky 40578

National Association of Wholesale-Distributors
600 S. Federal Street
Chicago, Illinois 60605

National Black MBA Association
111 E. Wacker Drive
Chicago, Illinois 60601

National Consumer Finance Association
1000 Sixteenth Street, NW
Washington, D.C. 20036

National Credit Union Management Association
  4989 Revel Trail, NW
  Atlanta, Georgia 30327

National Institute of Governmental Purchasing, Inc.
  115 Hillwood Avenue
  Falls Church, Virginia 22046

National Retail Merchants Association
  100 W. Thirty-first Street
  New York, New York 10001

National Society of Public Accountants
  1010 N. Fairfax Street
  Alexandria, Virginia 22314

Sales Promotion Executives Association
  2130 Delancey Street
  Philadelphia, Pennsylvania 19103

U.S. League of Savings Institutions
  1709 New York Avenue, NW
  Washington, D.C. 20006

U.S. Small Business Administration
  1441 L Street, NW
  Washington, D.C. 20416

Appendix C

THE MANY TITLES OF MANAGERS

Industry	Selected managerial job titles
Banks and credit agencies	Loan officer Trust officer Branch manager
Educational services	Dean Registrar Superintendent Principal Director of testing
Eating and drinking places	Manager, food service Manager, restaurant
Health services	Director of laboratories Nursing home administrator Public health administrator Hospital administrator

Business services	Manager, advertising agency
	Account executive
	Manager, electronic data
	  processing
	Manager, credit and
	  collection

Industry	*Selected managerial job titles*
Wholesale trade, durable goods	Manager, merchandise Manager, parts Distribution warehouse manager
Local government, except education and hospitals	Mayor Council member Clerk of court Assessor Park superintendent
Insurance	Manager, actuarial department Manager, investment department
Automotive dealers and gasoline service stations	Service manager Sales manager Manager, parts Manager, gasoline station
Miscellaneous retail stores	Manager, merchandise Retail store manager Aisle manager Floor supervisor
Food stores	Produce department manager Grocery department manager Meat department manager Store manager
Special trades contractors	Building mover Deep-well contractor Excavation contractor
Membership organizations	Association executive Membership secretary Treasurer
Wholesale, trade, nondurable goods	Market manager Textile conversion manager Manager, meat sales and storage Manager, tobacco warehouse Sales supervisor

Industry	*Selected managerial job titles*
Manufacturing	Plant manager Production planning manager Quality control manager Chief design engineer Export manager
Real estate	Manager, land development Property manager
Federal government	Member of Congress Postmaster Director of veterans' affairs Federal judge
General merchandise stores	Sales coordinator Fashion coordinator Merchandise manager Floor supervisor
Communications	Regulatory administrator Superintendent, substation Program director Radio and television director Public affairs director Cable supervisor
General contractors and operative builders	Construction superintendent Supervisor, bridges and buildings Railroad construction director Road supervisor
Apparel and accessory stores	Merchandise manager Floor supervisor Fashion coordinator
Electrical and electronic machinery and equipment	Plant manager Production planning manager Quality control manager Export manager Chief design engineer

Industry	Selected managerial job titles
Printing, publishing, and allied industries	Publisher Advertising manager Chief editor
Social services	Director of social services Welfare director Field administrator Director of group counseling
Miscellaneous services	Research-contracts supervisor Manager, land surveying
State government, except education and hospitals	Governor Legislator Directors of veterans' affairs State liquor commissioner Railroad commissioner
Personal services	Funeral director Launderette manager
Chemicals and allied products	Refinery superintendent Plant manager Production planning manager Quality control manager Chief design engineer Export manager
Food and kindred products	Brewing director General superintendent, milling Manager, food-processing plant
Transportation equipment	Superintendent, car construction Plant manager Production-planning manager Quality control manager Chief design engineer Export manager

RECOMMENDED READING

Admissions Guide to Selective Business Schools, Matthew May, NTC Publishing Group, Lincolnwood, Illinois, 1990.

Careers and the MBA, 1989 ed., Bob Adams Publishing.

Employment Policies: Looking to the Year 2000, National Alliance of Business, 1986.

Executive Jobs Unlimited, Carl R. Boll, Macmillan Publishing Company, New York, 1980.

How to Make the Right Career Moves, Deborah Perlmutter Bloch, NTC Publishing Group, Lincolnwood, Illinois, 1990.

In the Age of the Smart Machine: The Future of Work and Power, Shoshana Zuboff, Basic Books, New York, 1988.

The MBA Career—Moving on the Fast Track to Success, Eugene Bronstein and Robert Hirsch, Barron's Educational Series, Woodbury, New York, 1983.

MBA JOBS!—An Insider's Guide to the Companies that Hire MBAs, Marian Salzman and Nancy Marx, American Management Association, 1986.

The Official Guide to MBA Programs, Jodi C. Krasna, Educational Testing Service, Princeton, New Jersey, 1990.

Opportunities in Banking Careers, Adrian A. Paradis, NTC Publishing Group, Lincolnwood, Illinois, 1986.

Opportunities in Financial Careers, Michael J. Sumichrast and Dean A. Christ, NTC Publishing Group, Lincolnwood, Illinois, 1991.

Opportunities in International Business Careers, Jeffrey Arpan, NTC Publishing Group, Lincolnwood, Illinois, 1989.

Opportunities in Marketing Careers, Margery Steinberg, NTC Publishing Group, Lincolnwood, Illinois, 1988.

Peak Performers, C. Garfield, Avon Books, New York, 1986.

Projections 2000, Bureau of Labor Statistics Bulletin 2302, U.S. Department of Labor, Washington, D.C., 1988.

Understanding Computers—What Managers and Users Need to Know, 2d ed., Myles E. Walsh, John Wiley & Sons, New York, 1985.

VGM CAREER BOOKS

OPPORTUNITIES IN
Available in both paperback and hardbound editions

Accounting Careers
Acting Careers
Advertising Careers
Aerospace Careers
Agriculture Careers
Airline Careers
Animal and Pet Care
Appraising Valuation Science
Architecture
Automotive Service
Banking
Beauty Culture
Biological Sciences
Biotechnology Careers
Book Publishing Careers
Broadcasting Careers
Building Construction Trades
Business Communication Careers
Business Management
Cable Television
Carpentry Careers
Chemical Engineering
Chemistry Careers
Child Care Careers
Chiropractic Health Care
Civil Engineering Careers
Commercial Art and Graphic Design
Computer Aided Design and Computer Aided Mfg.
Computer Maintenance Careers
Computer Science Careers
Counseling & Development
Crafts Careers
Culinary Careers
Dance
Data Processing Careers
Dental Care
Drafting Careers
Electrical Trades
Electronic and Electrical Engineering
Energy Careers
Engineering Careers
Engineering Technology Careers
Environmental Careers
Eye Care Careers
Fashion Careers
Fast Food Careers
Federal Government Careers
Film Careers
Financial Careers
Fire Protection Services
Fitness Careers
Food Services
Foreign Language Careers
Forestry Careers
Gerontology Careers
Government Service
Graphic Communications
Health and Medical Careers
High Tech Careers
Home Economics Careers
Hospital Administration
Hotel & Motel Management
Human Resources Management Careers

Industrial Design
Information Systems Careers
Insurance Careers
Interior Design
International Business
Journalism Careers
Landscape Architecture
Laser Technology
Law Careers
Law Enforcement and Criminal Justice
Library and Information Science
Machine Trades
Magazine Publishing Careers
Management
Marine & Maritime Careers
Marketing Careers
Materials Science
Mechanical Engineering
Medical Technology Careers
Microelectronics
Military Careers
Modeling Careers
Music Careers
Newspaper Publishing Careers
Nursing Careers
Nutrition Careers
Occupational Therapy Careers
Office Occupations
Opticianry
Optometry
Packaging Science
Paralegal Careers
Paramedical Careers
Part-time & Summer Jobs
Performing Arts Careers
Petroleum Careers
Pharmacy Careers
Photography
Physical Therapy Careers
Physician Careers
Plumbing & Pipe Fitting
Podiatric Medicine
Printing Careers
Property Management Careers
Psychiatry
Psychology
Public Health Careers
Public Relations Careers
Purchasing Careers
Real Estate
Recreation and Leisure
Refrigeration and Air Conditioning Trades
Religious Service
Restaurant Careers
Retailing
Robotics Careers
Sales Careers
Sales & Marketing
Secretarial Careers
Securities Industry
Social Science Careers
Social Work Careers
Speech-Language Pathology Careers
Sports & Athletics
Sports Medicine
State and Local Government
Teaching Careers

Technical Communications
Telecommunications
Television and Video Careers
Theatrical Design & Production
Transportation Careers
Travel Careers
Veterinary Medicine Careers
Vocational and Technical Careers
Welding Careers
Word Processing
Writing Careers
Your Own Service Business

CAREERS IN
Accounting
Advertising
Business
Communications
Computers
Education
Engineering
Health Care
Science

CAREER DIRECTORIES
Careers Encyclopedia
Occupational Outlook Handbook

CAREER PLANNING
Admissions Guide to Selective Business Schools
Career Planning and Development for College Students and Recent Graduates
Careers Checklists
Careers for Bookworms and Other Literary Types
Careers for Sports Nuts
Handbook of Business and Management Careers
Handbook of Scientific and Technical Careers
How to Change Your Career
How to Get and Get Ahead On Your First Job
How to Get People to Do Things Your Way
How to Have a Winning Job Interview
How to Land a Better Job
How to Make the Right Career Moves
How to Prepare for College
How to Run Your Own Home Business
How to Write a Winning Résumé
Joyce Lain Kennedy's Career Book
Life Plan
Planning Your Career of Tomorrow
Planning Your College Education
Planning Your Military Career
Planning Your Young Child's Education

SURVIVAL GUIDES
Dropping Out or Hanging In
High School Survival Guide
College Survival Guide

VGM Career Horizons
a division of NTC *Publishing Group*
4255 West Touhy Avenue
Lincolnwood, Illinois 60646-1975